a nanking winter

a nanking winter

marjorie chan

Playwrights Canada Press
Toronto • Canada

Playwrights Canada Press
The Canadian Drama Publisher
215 Spadina Ave., Suite 230, Toronto, Ontario, Canada, M5T 2C7
phone 416.703.0013 fax 416.408.3402
orders@playwrightscanada.com • www.playwrightscanada.com

For professional or amateur production rights, please contact
Great North Artists Management
350 Dupont St., Toronto, Ontario, Canada, M5R 1V9
phone 416.925.2051 fax 416.925.3904

The publisher acknowledges the support of the Canadian taxpayers through the Government
of Canada Book Publishing Industry Development Program, the Canada Council for the
Arts, the Ontario Arts Council, and the Ontario Media Development Corporation.

Cover image of Ginling College courtesy of Special Collections, Yale Divinity School Library
Production Editor and Cover Design: Micheline Courtemanche

Library and Archives Canada Cataloguing in Publication

Chan, Marjorie
A Nanking winter / Marjorie Chan.

A play.
ISBN 978-0-88754-863-5

1. Nanking Massacre, Nanjing, Jiangsu Sheng, China, 1937--Drama.
I. Title.

PS8605.H355N36 2009   C812'.6   C2009-900109-8

First edition: February 2009
Printed and bound by Canadian Printco at Scarborough, Canada.

for iris

contents

introduction

In my view, *a nanking winter* is cubism disguised as realism. On first reading it seems like a straightforward retelling of a horrific event and its effect on a writer in the present. Closer inspection, however, reveals it as a kaleidoscopic examination of the importance and consequence of truth.

Like any good storyteller, Marjorie Chan insists on the scope and breadth of her tale. She tenaciously sets her play in the past and the present and on two continents. She gives full voice to a difficult character, the ferocious and unwieldy Irene Wu, a writer haunted by a forgotten holocaust. She imagines a small group of unlikely heroes in the centre of the horror, one who is killed, one who commits suicide, one who is ultimately silenced (Niklas is a pariah on his return to Germany) and one who survives to tell the story.

With this, Marjorie asks her questions. Who controls history? What is the impulse to deny that rape is used as a weapon of war? Do we in the West fashion stories to ensure our role as protagonist (or hero if you prefer)? And ultimately—what happens to the truth-tellers?

Structurally, Marjorie takes on the large task of portraying the past and the present by dividing the play in two. This does not, however, prevent it from being one dramatic event. Irene, outraged by the brutality of the invasion and the ease in which it has been covered up, fills her book with facts. As she insists we digest important details, opening us up to experience viscerally the random and hellish savagery of the event. We follow the lives of Little Mei, Big Mei, Anna and Niklas at Ginling College with Irene's voice in our head. In this way, the play loops back upon itself, completing the circle while shattering into many pieces. At the end we are back where we started— with bravery, with Irene's story.

a nanking winter urges us to remember the 1937 invasion of Nanking by the Japanese Imperial Army and the subsequent horror inflicted on its citizens. It reminds us also that unthinkable brutality occurs during all wars, that we should make our choices with eyes open when it comes to our role in the world. The ongoing cover-up of what happened in Nanking reminds us of how power can rewrite history.

With Iris Chang, Minnie Vautrin and John Rabe as inspiration, Marjorie Chan champions those who insist on telling the truth and recognizes the sacrifice in doing so.

Ruth Madoc-Jones, Director
Toronto, 2008

playwright's notes

The invasion of Nanking is an historical event and I encourage readers to research the era on their own terms. My play is an interpretation of these events and as such there are variances, especially in regards to the historical timeline. These are deliberate choices for dramatic intent. There are also three historical figures that served as inspiration and starting points. My depiction of these characters should under no circumstances be considered anything resembling historical. Their personalities and their lives are pure conjecture.

Irene Wu is inspired very loosely by the life of writer Iris Chang (1968–2004) who wrote the controversial book *The Rape of Nanking: The Forgotten Holocaust*. She died by her own hand at the side of a California Highway on November 9, 2004.

Anna Mallery is inspired by Minnie Vautrin (1886–1941), an American missionary who spent over thirty years in China. She eventually had to return to the United States because of her failing mental state. She died by her own hand by releasing gas into her home on May 16, 1941.

Niklas Hermann is inspired by German businessman and the highest ranking Nazi in Nanking, John Rabe (1882–1950). After returning to Germany to solicit an audience for his documents, he became a pariah and died impoverished on January 5, 1949.

language

Act One is in English as written.

Act Two has some variations. When Niklas, Anna and Hiro Fukuyama are speaking together, they are assumed to be speaking English. When Niklas and Anna converse with the girls, they are assumed to be speaking Chinese (Mandarin). There are occasional references to language switches to communicate this choice to the audience. This is not historically accurate, but a simplification for the stage.

acknowledgements

The playwright gratefully acknowledges the following organizations for their assistance in development:

2007 Banff Playwrights Colony (a partnership between the Canada Council for the Arts, The Banff Centre and Alberta Theatre Projects), Nightwood Theatre (2006 and 2007 Groundswell Festivals), Ontario Arts Council (Theatre Creators' Reserve — Native Earth Performing Arts) and Cahoots Theatre Projects.

Many thanks to the workshop participants:

Ella Chan, Grace Lynn Kung, John Ng, Kate Hennig, Bruce Hunter, Daniela Vlaskalic, Rylan Wilkie, Adrienne Smook, Val Pearson, Brian Dooley, Kira Bradley, Brooke Johnson, Hardee Lineham, Keira Loughran, Siobhan Richardson, Stephen Russell and especially dramaturge Ruth Madoc-Jones.

Special thanks to Toronto ALPHA for their assistance while the playwright was in Nanjing, China.

a nanking winter was first produced by Nightwood Theatre, in association with Cahoots Theatre Projects, premiering at the Factory Theatre Mainstage, Toronto, February 27, 2008, with the following company:

KURT/HIRO Fukuyama/ ZHANG/SOLDIER	Leon Aureus
AUDREY/BIG MEI	Ella Chan
JULIA/ANNA Mallery	Brooke Johnson
IRENE/LITTLE MEI	Grace Lynn Kung
FRANK/NIKLAS Hermann	Stephen Russell

Director and Dramaturge: Ruth Madoc-Jones
Set and Costume Designer: Camellia Koo
Lighting Designer: Renée Brode
Music and Sound Designer: Rick Hyslop
Stage Manager: Melanie Klodt
Assistant Director: Esther Jun
Assistant Designer: Anna Treusch
Apprentice Stage Manager: Stephanie Nakamura
Production Manager: Matt Farrell
Production Assistant: Deborah A. Catriona
Head of Wardrobe: Jung Hye Kim
Wardrobe and Props Assistant: Natalie Moore
Props Advisor: David Hoekstra
Fight Director: Joe Bostick

characters

Act One – Present – November 2004 – California

IRENE WU, a writer of Chinese descent in her thirties
AUDREY WU, her sister, an artist, in her twenties or thirties
KURT Tagasaki, Irene's husband, of Japanese descent, in his thirties
JULIA, Irene's publisher
FRANK, a lawyer from the publishing house

Act Two – Past – December 1937 – Nanking

LITTLE MEI, a Chinese orphan, also known as Mei-Mei,
        in her early twenties
BIG MEI, a young pregnant resident of Nanking, late teens
        (also plays GIRL TWO)
HIRO Fukuyama, a Japanese diplomat, in his thirties
        (also plays ZHANG and the SOLDIER)
ANNA Mallery, an American Catholic missionary in China,
        in her forties (also plays GIRL ONE)
NIKLAS Hermann, the highest ranking Nazi officer in China,
        in his fifties or sixties

Played by five actors, doubled as follows:

IRENE and LITTLE MEI
AUDREY and BIG MEI
KURT, HIRO Fukuyama, ZHANG and SOLDIER*
JULIA and ANNA Mallery
FRANK and NIKLAS Hermann

* Possibly a sixth actor (male, Asian) could take on the roles of ZHANG and
   the SOLDIER in Act Two, if desired.

prologue

Lights up. IRENE with her hair or face wet, seemingly naked in a bathtub or in a tight spot with the sound of the shower or water running. She delivers her speech to the audience calmly and simply. In the air she draws a heart as if on steamed glass.

IRENE   As a child,
Whenever I drew a person,
First I drew their heart, and coloured it in red.
Everything else was black and white.

As a child, only three
Crawling where I shouldn't have been,
Along a river, beside the campgrounds
I fell and scraped my knee raw.

There was blood
And my mother scolded me.
Clean it, she said.
It won't heal unless you clean it.

She held my knee under the water
And clear it was,
Clear enough to see the blood flowing from me.

As a child, and it being red, I thought
It was my heart bleeding.
I watched my heart flow and it would not stop.
I thought it would never stop.

I asked my mother
How can one heart hold so much?

act one

california, 2004

Lights up on an open sunny living room. It's wide and bright, West Coast furniture in warm woods; it makes us feel safe. There are the following entrances: front door, basement office, bathroom and kitchen. The front door opens and KURT enters, carrying a bag with bottles in it. He looks around.

KURT   Irene! Irene?

IRENE   *(off)* I'm in the office!

KURT   What's all this stuff?

> *IRENE enters, bringing boxes up from the basement office.*

IRENE   I'm trying to get a head start on it.

KURT   People are coming.

IRENE   I know.

> *A beat.*

I came back from my walk and you were gone.

KURT   I know, sorry. I didn't want to be late.

IRENE   I thought you were going to wait for me…

KURT   Look, I got some champagne from the restaurant! We'll crack it open later…

> *He crosses to the kitchen.*

IRENE   It's not going to be a party, is it? I said no parties, Kurt.

> *KURT re-enters.*

KURT   Well… it was leftover from a corporate event. It'll screw up the accounting, but who cares? My parents put me in charge…

IRENE   They get off okay?

KURT Yeah, but my mother's luggage was over the limit. I don't know why she brings everything, you can get anything you want in Tokyo.

IRENE I would've come to the airport to say goodbye.

KURT No, no it's okay. You didn't… you didn't really want to. You're busy.

IRENE Yes, but—I'm willing to talk about it. I've said that a million times. I want to talk about it.

KURT Yeah, but they don't want to talk about it.

> *Beat.*

IRENE Here. I wanted to give this back to your mother, and thank her. Thank her for letting me look at it.

> *From the boxes, IRENE hands KURT a picture frame. It is a black and white portrait. A beat.*

KURT Don't…

IRENE I didn't say anything.

> *A beat.*

KURT My parents have to go, Irene. They go to Yasukuni [1] every year. This is how they honour my grandfather.

IRENE Okay. *(beat)* But what if—

KURT Irene.

IRENE What if my parents worshipped at a shrine, that also honoured… I don't know… Hitler? What would you think of that?

KURT Hitler is not enshrined in Yasukuni.

IRENE What if he was? How is it different?

KURT The shrine is for those that served Japan in war.

IRENE And some of them, a little over a thousand of them, just happen to be convicted war criminals!

KURT Irene. No.

---

1 A Shinto shrine of considerable controversy, honouring those that died in war serving Imperial Japan. Enshrined at the site are one thousand, sixty-eight people convicted by an international tribunal of war crimes, including twelve Class A war criminals, as well as two more charged with Class A crimes, but who died before trial.

IRENE   No, they're not convicted war criminals?

KURT   My parents are engaged in a private act. A private act to honour my grandfather.

IRENE   Please.

KURT   Why are you making this harder than it has to be?

IRENE   I can't ignore the fact that your grandfather—

KURT   You don't know, Irene, you weren't there, you don't know.

IRENE   I don't?

KURT   You don't see how difficult it is for me? For my family?

IRENE   What—so, I'm not a part of your family!

>   *Beat.*

KURT   Look, my grandfather, my grandfather… he was like any other grandfather. He spoiled us, snuck us candy before dinner and let us get away with murder. I can remember hanging out with him on the beach. Japanese beaches aren't like the beaches here. The sand isn't white. It's black. It's black because it's made of volcanic rock. And because it's so dark, it makes it really hot to walk on. So whenever it got too hot, my grandfather would take my hand and we'd run into the ocean to cool our feet. But in the water, there were jellyfish, lots of them. And they'd sting you! I got stung so many times, I can't even tell you! So really, you had no choice. Out into the water to be stung by jellyfish or onto the beach and have your feet scorched! You had to keep going back and forth. If you stood still in one place, you were done for. That's how I remember him, not being able to stand still, not being able to choose.

>   *Beat.*

(looking at the picture) He's so young here.

>   *The doorbell rings.*

IRENE   I don't want to see anyone yet.

KURT   Irene, what about all the stuff—

>   *The doorbell rings again. IRENE exits to the office. KURT goes to the door and AUDREY bursts in.*

AUDREY   *(entering)* Hey!

KURT   Hi Audrey.

AUDREY   Where is everyone? Kurt—where is everyone?

KURT   They haven't arrived yet. Actually there's only gonna be—

AUDREY   Where is she? Is she freaking out? *(calling into the house)* Irene! Are you freaking out?

IRENE   *(off)* Go away, Audrey!

AUDREY   Yikes. She's totally freaking out!

KURT   Why don't you take off your— Why don't you have a coat?

AUDREY   I mean, why shouldn't she freak out? It's so great, y'know, really fantastic, just really, really a great thing! I mean a book! A book! I always knew she had it in her! Omigod, I have to sit down.

KURT   Then sit so we can talk. Sit.

AUDREY   Oh, I can't sit. It's too much!

KURT   Look, I'll make you some tea, 'kay?

AUDREY   Sure, sure. But not caffeinated, not green tea 'kay? Like after your anniversary party, I was totally buzzing, flying all night. Oh my god, I am such a basket case on that stuff, so no green tea for me!

KURT   What kind of tea do you want then?

AUDREY   Whatever. I'm easy. Organic if you got it.

     As KURT tries to go.

Where is everyone?

KURT   *(popping back in)* It's only going to be us and Julia… and she's bringing someone else…

AUDREY   That's it?

KURT   It's not a party or anything.

AUDREY   Julia said if I came, I'd get a book, so I thought it was a party or something—

KURT   The launch is tomorrow—

AUDREY   But Julia said I'd get a copy—because seriously, I am so strapped right now, it is not even funny. Don't tell Irene I'm broke!

KURT   Okay—

AUDREY   So where are the books?

KURT   There was a bit of a complication—

AUDREY   What complication?

KURT   I'll explain. Let me just put some water on. Just, wait—

He goes.

AUDREY   *(calling)* What complication?

A cell phone rings. It should ring long enough so the audience even shuffles a bit, maybe even turn their own off. It should be just a normal ring but distinctive. AUDREY looks around but doesn't otherwise react.

Phone!

It rings some more. AUDREY looks around.

KURT   *(off)* Can you get it?

AUDREY   What?

KURT   *(off)* It's Irene's!

AUDREY walks over to the basement entrance, calling down.

AUDREY   Irene! Your phone!

IRENE   *(off)* Leave it!

KURT   *(off)* Can you get it?

IRENE   *(off)* Leave it!

AUDREY   Where is it?

Still ringing.

KURT   *(off)* Get it, it might be Julia.

AUDREY   Where is it?

Just as she finds and answers it, KURT enters.

Hello?… No, this is her sister. Who's calling?… Who's calling please?… Hello? What? Hello?

> *She hangs up the phone. Seeing KURT's expression, she*
> *downplays it.*

(deliberately casual) Stupid kids.

KURT   Shit. We'll have to change the number again. Don't tell her about the call, okay?

AUDREY   I'm sure it's not going to be a surprise.

KURT   Just promise, okay, Audrey? Don't talk to her about it. Let me do it?

AUDREY   If she's not worried 'bout the calls, I don't know why we should be! It comes with the territory; if you write a book that pushes people's buttons… people are going to push back.

> *IRENE enters from the basement, carrying another box of files.*

Hey!

IRENE   Why is she here? Why is my sister here?

AUDREY   It's Irene Wu! The Published Writer!

IRENE   It's not a party, is it?

KURT   No, no.

IRENE   I specifically asked for no party. It's bad enough I have to do the promo stuff. I don't want parties in my own home.

KURT   It's not a party. I mean Julia's coming and she might bring someone…

IRENE   Who?

KURT   Anyway, don't worry 'bout it. Audrey's… Audrey's early.

AUDREY   For once in my life!

IRENE   Who called?

AUDREY   Uhhh… nobody!

KURT   Nobody.

> *IRENE looks at them both.*

IRENE   You better not be keeping anything from me.

> *She exits.*

AUDREY   See? She's not worried, I'm not worried!

KURT   All of this started on our trip to Asia. I knew we shouldn't have gone! During the whole trip, I tell you, we were being harassed everywhere we went! Not just Japan, China too! We had this one interview lined up with a survivor in Nanjing.[2] When we show up at her apartment she denies she was even there during the invasion! We show her a picture of herself in the same apartment in 1937, she still denies it! You know what? Someone got to her! Why else would she agree to an interview and then deny everything?

AUDREY   Um—maybe she was ashamed? Maybe she didn't want people to know she was raped? I mean, omigod, can you imagine?

KURT   No, I can't. I can't. I don't know. How can you know? How can you know what you would do? Irene says that the rapes were systematic and deliberate but I just don't know. War is messy. Bad shit happens. The violation of women is tragic, yes. But calculated? I don't know. I've never been in a war… neither has Irene.

> *Beat.*

Do you wanna know why we came back early? In Tokyo, there were small vans that followed us. When we got out, they got out. They would chant and wave their signs. It was all polite, but vocal and insistent. Then in this *ryokan*, I mean nice hotel, really nice. But— we were having tea before dinner and Irene started to feel sick. I mean, really sick and very, very quickly. Just her, not me. She was vomiting within minutes.

AUDREY   I didn't know that!

KURT   Irene didn't want you to know. Anyway, after she recovered, we caught the next flight out. It was then she told me that her tea in the *ryokan* tasted bitter.

AUDREY   What? What are you saying?

KURT   Maybe it's the same people calling her, trying to harass her!

AUDREY   Wait, wait, wait. So these fanatics, they want her to stop writing about Nanking. So—they call her names on the internet, they follow her around and then they try and poison her?

KURT   Yes.

---

2 The name of the city in 1937 was Nanking, but it is presently known as Nanjing.

AUDREY   And then what? When that doesn't work—they crank call her?

KURT   Maybe they're planning something worse!

AUDREY   Kurt—c'mon!

KURT   This is why, okay, why we have to take precautions... look out for her...

AUDREY   Yeah. Of course. This time, of course.

KURT   No Audrey, I mean it. We want to try to pre-empt any kind of, y'know, ammunition...

AUDREY   What are you talking about?

KURT   I'm trying to explain something.

AUDREY   What?

KURT   I'm trying to explain a decision, a hard decision! It was in Irene's interest. With her best interests at heart.

AUDREY   What the fuck are you talking about, Kurt?

IRENE enters, this time with more boxes of stuff.

IRENE   Help me.

AUDREY   This is your research! What are you doing with it?

IRENE   *(to AUDREY)* Maybe I'll give it to you!

AUDREY   What am I going to do with it?

IRENE   Anything you want. I'm done. Finished.

KURT   Really?

IRENE   Yup.

KURT   You're done? That's a great step, Irene, that's great.

IRENE   Did the books come?

KURT   Julia said she worked it all out.

IRENE   Ridiculous. Night before it hits the shelves, I still haven't even seen it! This whole process has been plagued with such... disrespect.

AUDREY   What happened to them?

IRENE   I don't even know! Some protests or something.

KURT   Well, Julia says she's bringing copies.

IRENE   Well, she "said" a lot of things! Anyone can "say" things! Especially to a writer on her first commission!

AUDREY   What's wrong with Julia?

KURT   Julia's great.

IRENE   Julia is patronizing. Julia is everything that's wrong about publishing. Julia wants to be some kind of maternal figure. I don't need a mother! I need someone who will stand up for my book!

KURT   She's given you a huge opportunity… and she knows, she knows books.

IRENE   She knows how to sell books. She knows how to manipulate writers. She knows how to take advantage of—

KURT   Stop it! You can't blame her because there's been "complications." It's not her fault you got… you… you…

IRENE   "You…" what Kurt? What were you going to say? "It's not her fault that I…"?

> *Beat.*

KURT   Did you get enough sleep last night?

IRENE   Don't.

KURT   What time did you go to bed?

IRENE   I said don't.

KURT   You're not getting enough rest. The doctors said rest is very important.

IRENE   I know what the doctors said. I was there when the doctors said it.

KURT   Well, sometimes you forget.

IRENE   I don't forget, Kurt. You don't think that if I could sleep, I would? You think that I choose to stay up all night?

AUDREY   Did you stay up all night?

IRENE   Yes, Audrey. And talking to you two about it stresses me out even more.

AUDREY   Just asking!

IRENE   Well, quit it. I can't stand the nagging.

AUDREY   He started it.

KURT   I'm not nagging.

IRENE   Don't. Okay? Don't worry 'bout me.

She exits back down to the basement again.

KURT   I'm trying to help her! I cook for her. I clean for her.

AUDREY   I don't think she wants a servant, Kurt.

KURT   I don't know what else to do. Look at all this crap! Goddammit!

He kicks one of the boxes. AUDREY moves a box out of his way. She picks up a photo and examines it.

AUDREY   Geez, she's practically the same age as me... *(looking closer)* How would you even do that? Bayonet?

KURT   Sword, probably.

AUDREY   These are horrible. No wonder she can't sleep.

KURT   Don't look at them... you won't forget them, if you look at them.

Beat.

AUDREY   She wouldn't try again—would she?

KURT   God, I don't know. I don't know...

Beat.

...that was the worst day of my life, finding her...

Beat.

You have to help today, okay Audrey? We need your help. It's really great that you're here. Whatever happens, try and keep Irene calm, okay?

AUDREY   What's going to happen?

KURT   Nothing. Nothing.

Beat.

Hey, y'know the doctors changed her prescription again. I think she's turned a corner, y'know? Those other drugs made her into such a zombie. But this one…. She's more like herself again. She's fiery, like she used to be… like when we first met in school and she was starting out at the paper… before all the stuff with the book…. Anyway, you haven't noticed?

AUDREY   Well, as long as she takes them—

The cell phone rings again. AUDREY goes to answer it.

Hello—

KURT   Give it to me. Give it to me.

She does and KURT roughly ends the call.

AUDREY   Kurt! What's the matter with you? What if it was someone important—

Again the phone rings.

KURT   Fucking assholes!

KURT roughly slams it shut. For good measure, he removes the battery and chucks the whole thing across the room. The kettle goes and KURT starts to storm off into the kitchen, just as IRENE enters with more stuff.

Goddammit!

KURT exits.

IRENE   What happened?

AUDREY   I don't know. Should I go talk to him?

IRENE   No. No. I hope he's not cooking. I said no party.

AUDREY   There's always a party round me!

IRENE   Yeah. Too much of a party.

A moment.

Did you talk to Comic Book Boy?

AUDREY   Don't call him that! And they're called graphic novels.

IRENE   Did you talk to him?

AUDREY   Uh-huh.

IRENE   And?

AUDREY   And… I'm going to keep it.

IRENE   And him?

AUDREY   Well, we're not getting married, that's for sure…

IRENE   But?

AUDREY   He said he'll be around.

IRENE   What about money? What are you going to do?

AUDREY   I have a sister with a bestseller coming out! I don't to have to worry!

IRENE   What are you going to do?

AUDREY   I don't know, okay. I'll figure it out later.

IRENE   Audrey.

AUDREY   Irene!

      A beat.

You're lucky you have Kurt, y'know. He's really proud of you. And maybe he just wants to see the end of it. Now that it's being released, you know you can move onto other stuff…

IRENE   Less controversial stuff?

AUDREY   I didn't say that.

IRENE   Did Kurt say that?

      No answer.

AUDREY   When… when I tried to bring you the copy to approve, well, y'know, while you were away—

IRENE   Don't say "away." Say hospital, or institution, or looney bin or whatever, just don't say "away." "Away" is at Lake Tahoe or on a cruise.

AUDREY   Well, when you were in the hospital… the book was due! It was nuts! And Julia and Hartford & Ross, they were really pressuring us. Kurt and me… and I couldn't really take it. I couldn't. So that's why I took off to San Fran. Look, I know I wasn't there for you. But Kurt was, he was there for you, okay? I mean, at one point, I think the company was going to pull it, but he wouldn't let them. And it was so hard, like, his family really came down on him, but he stuck up for you!

IRENE   I know.

AUDREY   I mean, is it better now 'tween you? Like, it seems like you guys are talking 'bout stuff?

IRENE   Yeah we talk. We talk in abstracts. We try.

AUDREY   Yeah… so?

IRENE   So?

> *Beat.*

AUDREY   Was Kurt's grandfather in Nanking?

IRENE   Not according to Kurt.

> *IRENE notices the phone carnage.*

What happened to my phone?

AUDREY   Kurt said he was going to tell you later. If he asks, I didn't tell you.

> *IRENE picks up her phone.*

IRENE   Couldn't he have just turned it off?

> *AUDREY finds the battery and IRENE starts to put it back together.*

He's overreacting. It's just some kids.

AUDREY   So you're not worried or anything?

IRENE   Why should I be worried? They can't hurt me over the phone!

> *IRENE checks her phone panel for messages.*

Hartford, probably. With another interview.

AUDREY   I know you said no party—but you didn't say no presents.

IRENE   Audrey… no.

AUDREY   Audrey yes! I made it myself! Damn, it's in the car, I'll go get it…

IRENE   You didn't have to get me anything.

AUDREY   I'll be right back!

IRENE   Audrey, where's your coat? It's freezing!

> *But she's gone. IRENE sits, tired and defeated, and for the moment alone. She looks around at all the boxes and, overwhelmed, she puts her face in her hands, closing her eyes. She stays here for a bit. KURT enters with tea. Seeing her, he places it down quickly and holds her. She lets him.*

KURT   Hey…. Hey…. Shhhh…. C'mon…. Look at me? Look at me. Irene… c'mon. You're okay…. Look at me…

> *She finally does.*

IRENE   I'm packed. I mean, most of my clothes. I've packed them.

KURT   Okay, it's okay. Don't worry.

IRENE   So when I go on the book tour, you know you can decide what you want to do, okay? If you want to stay here, or—

KURT   I won't sell the house, until you're sure, okay? This stuff can wait, you know, until you get back…

IRENE   I'll try to finish my office today. After everyone leaves…

KURT   Don't worry about it. Leave it. We can talk about all our things and what we're going to do—we can talk about this later—okay?

> *The front door flies opens. AUDREY enters with JULIA and FRANK.*

AUDREY   Look who I found outside! Oh it's freezing out there!

JULIA   Irene!

FRANK   Hello. Congratulations.

JULIA   Oh darling, congratulations. It's truly exciting. This is Frank.

FRANK   Nice to meet you.

IRENE   Let me take your coats. You met my sister Audrey?

FRANK   Yes, outside.

IRENE   This is Kurt.

AUDREY   Oh it's so cold. Brr.

KURT   Hi Julia. Frank.

JULIA   I've been here a million times, but I always forget the house number.

AUDREY   They were wandering up and down the street.

FRANK   We tried to call.

JULIA   We called your cell.

AUDREY   You did? Did I answer? Was it me? I'm so sorry. It wasn't me, was it?

FRANK   No, no it wasn't you.

JULIA   No one answered. Nobody! We called twice.

IRENE   Sorry. My phone… I think I'm having problems again.

JULIA   Really? Not again.

IRENE   I think so.

KURT   Someone kept calling today. Some blocked number.

FRANK   I'm afraid that might've been me, my phone.

JULIA   We called. We were lost.

AUDREY   They were just wandering up and down the street.

JULIA   We called but no one answered. We called twice.

KURT   Oh.

IRENE   Well, you're here now.

KURT   Yes, welcome.

IRENE   Yes, have some tea. It's… what kind is it, Kurt?

KURT   It's vanilla something.

AUDREY   I hope there's no caffeine in it!

FRANK   So Irene. Are you anxious to see it?

IRENE   Oh of course. I've seen a mock-up…

FRANK   Your first book, right?

IRENE   Yes.

FRANK   Quite a topic. Certainly opened my eyes to the situation.

IRENE   You read it?

FRANK   Interesting all the Europeans and Americans in Nanking at the time of the Japanese invasion.

IRENE   Yes, there were quite a few. This was pre-World War II. Nanking was the capital in 1937, so there was quite a bit of international trade. And of course, a lot of foreigners escaped Shanghai when the Japanese came.

FRANK   Only to have Nanking invaded!

IRENE   Yes.

FRANK   Poor bastards. Lucky for the Chinese we were there.

AUDREY   Where are the books? Are they in your car?

JULIA   Oh no no no, the company's sending them here. No worries, no worries. I saw the finished cover, they look great. They'll look fantastic! And I know they finally shipped out to stores yesterday. Kurt explained? It was just a delay.

IRENE   What exactly happened?

JULIA   Does it even matter? Look, I don't want you to worry your little head. A little controversy never hurt a new writer.

FRANK   Especially one writing non-fiction!

JULIA   The books'll be here soon enough.

FRANK   Good. Gotta pick up my kid by eight. My week with him. His mother goes bitch-crazy when I don't pick him up on time.

JULIA   Frank… please.

FRANK   *(continuing)* I mean, she works from home, what difference does it make?

JULIA   So! Have you two packed and got your things sorted?

          A beat.

IRENE   Excuse me?

JULIA   For the book tour?

IRENE   Oh. Kurt's not coming on the tour.

JULIA   He's not?

KURT   Actually, my parents'll probably retire in Japan so I'm back at the restaurant full-time.

JULIA   Okay.

> *JULIA and FRANK look at each other.*

It's just, you do realize, it's quite a long tour, you're lucky to get it. Fourteen dates across North America, starting here and moving east…

IRENE   And you'll be coming?

JULIA   Of course! Not in every city. But, definitely. Definitely. I'll definitely try. It's only—well—are you comfortable travelling all by yourself?

IRENE   I don't need a babysitter.

JULIA   I wasn't suggesting you did! I thought you might want a companion. Maybe Audrey? Hartford's pulling out all the stops, first class hotels, first class airfare. Lots of time for sightseeing.

AUDREY   Wow.

JULIA   Audrey, what do you say? You never know, we may even get over the pond! Hartford's still working out the details, but translations are on the way. Strong interest, very strong interest. German, definitely, obviously. French. Danish interest for some reason! UK version, but I told you that already…

IRENE   Mandarin? Cantonese?

JULIA   Well…

IRENE   Korean?

JULIA   Irene—

IRENE   Japanese?

JULIA   No.

IRENE   No Asian translations?

JULIA   Listen, we do a North American run, and, and Europe looks pretty good, promising. And… it's a delay in Asia, that's all. After they see the sales, they won't need convincing. We don't want to release the book without the proper research into the market. We research, we wait, and the book is released in the proper climate. You don't want your book to be a bust, do you? And we certainly don't want a repeat of your last time in Japan.

KURT No, I agree.

JULIA You are not a complete unknown in these circles. They have been misquoting your articles for years!

IRENE I was a business reporter.

JULIA Who occasionally strayed into cultural territory in her pieces. Which brought you to my attention.

IRENE So it's my fault?

JULIA So we want to be careful how we proceed.

FRANK Very careful.

JULIA eyes FRANK.

JULIA Hartford's going to be very happy. And very happy to have you along... Audrey?

AUDREY Okay! It's not like I'm doing anything else!

JULIA Okay!

IRENE So, I guess I don't have a say!

JULIA Irene— It'll be lovely. A lovely tour. You know, the publishers are really behind you. They believe in you and what you're trying to say. They're gonna promote the hell outta this book, don't you worry. Hartford & Ross wants everyone who's anyone to have your name on their lips. We want every major paper to review your book. We want it taught in universities. We want you booked into every talk show, every discussion panel. We want you to be the go-to Chinese writer.

IRENE For what? For everything?

JULIA No, no. Of course not. Not everything. Relevant things naturally. Political things, women's issues, you know, Darfur or even the Bosnian women, Pakistan...

IRENE I'm not a specialist in any of those areas...

JULIA Well, you don't have to be a specialist to be on a panel! That's the whole point. They start the conversation about genocide or some such thing and from there, you cite an example from your book and talk about Nanking blah blah blah. Get it? Now, you've mentioned

your book—and someone somewhere out there in TV land—
someone will go out and buy it!

IRENE   Okay.

FRANK   Well, no, you can't just go out there and say anything!

JULIA   No, of course, no no no. That's not what I meant. No, you
most definitely can't—

FRANK   So tomorrow, we'll meet early, with my team, and we'll go
over a few things. Lines of argument, phrasing, that kind of thing.

IRENE   What?

FRANK   If you're really concerned, we can email you our notes.
I mean, it's all your material, we've just organized quotations, direct
from your book. Mind you, we've organized them into arguments.
We do it for all our non-fiction writers. Sometimes we have to do it
for our fiction writers too, don't we?

IRENE   I don't understand, Frank. Who, who are you?

FRANK   Didn't she tell you? Didn't she tell you why I'm here?

JULIA   I haven't had the chance…

FRANK   Frank Sadowitch, Hartford & Ross & Company. Legal
Department.

IRENE   Oh.

FRANK   You do understand, right, that a book that is as controversial
as yours—there are things that raise a few eyebrows. For starters,
your accusations towards the current Japanese government and
the royal family!

IRENE   I was very thorough, Mr. Sadowitch. My references,
my research—

FRANK   Yes, your research. Very impressive. We went through your
book with a fine-toothed comb. I tell ya, I wasn't sure though. That
first draft I read. I thought, a Nazi hero, what the fuck!

IRENE   Okay…

FRANK   Sorry. Never start talking about Nazis in polite company,
it's bound to go badly.

JULIA   Frank—

Brooke Johnson and Stephen Russell
photo by Guntar Kravis

FRANK   But I mean, he was a Nazi for god's sake!

IRENE   Niklas Hermann was de-nazified just before he died. In fact, in his diaries, he says that—

FRANK   Discovering his diary! Now, that—is priceless! Good thing his son let you have it!

IRENE   He didn't initially. Until he trusted me. I had to go back day after day.

FRANK   I mean the amount of research that you recovered—the diary, the secret photos, the letters to Hitler! What a great story. It'd make a great movie.

JULIA   Oh yeah! A movie!

FRANK   You could call it "Nazi of Nanking"!

JULIA   Or maybe "Niklas of Nanking…"

FRANK   And then that American woman…. What was her name? The missionary… the Sister who taught at the college… Gin-a-ling.

IRENE   Ginling College. Her name was Anna Mallery.

FRANK   Anna Mallery—is that not a name for a movie character or what? And talk about tragic! Her life was tragic! Now that's an ending! You could call that movie "Nun of Nanking"! Make a whole series!

JULIA   Frank…

FRANK   "Nicky and the Nun"!

IRENE   *(a correction)* Anna Mallery and Niklas Hermann are both considered heroes in China. They were at the centre of the entire safety zone operation, saving thousands of lives.

FRANK   I'm just happy you decided to beef up those sections. It made a huge shift for me, in terms of the growth of your book. A huge shift. I mean, without it… I don't know too much about Sino-Japanese relations and all. It's a big blur. But you get the foreign nationals in— gives me a focus for the story—

IRENE   It's not a story. It's not fiction.

JULIA   You know what he means—a narrative approach to non-fiction… shaping the information in a way that engages your audience. You have to know your audience! Academics, historians and Chinese advocates, yes, fine, a very small market. But, including the Western witnesses gives your book better range and broader appeal!

IRENE   What?!

JULIA   You want to tell this story, right? Well, when you're able to tell it from a Western point of view—this is the English reader after all, this is where the market is—

IRENE   Wait. Wait. Let me just get this straight. You're saying that it's good that I included the foreigners because *it will sell more books!?*

JULIA   No, not just that. That wasn't what I was saying at all!

IRENE   So what are you saying?

FRANK   Telling the truth is a good thing. Telling the truth about the Americans and Germans, yes even Nazis, who were able to save the Chinese people—

IRENE They saved *some* Chinese people. They didn't save *the* Chinese people.

FRANK You didn't let me finish. The Chinese people of Nanking. The Westerners set up the safety zone didn't they? That's what your research says?

IRENE Yes, of course…

FRANK At great risk to their own lives?

IRENE Right—but—

FRANK And what was the Chinese army doing? What were the officials of Nanking doing?

IRENE They were being invaded!

FRANK And weren't they also in retreat from the city? Leaving it virtually defenceless? In your book, you said that the Chinese army was ill-equipped and unprepared. That they were ineffective! Didn't you write that? I didn't write that.

IRENE But the Chinese didn't have the power! Niklas Hermann had influence because of the colour of his skin, the swastika on his sleeve. That meant something to the Japanese.

FRANK I think we're saying the same thing, aren't we?

IRENE No, I don't think we are! You're saying that representing these Western heroes with prominence is a way to make it more palatable for a Western audience.

JULIA Irene—now don't get—

IRENE That it's more convenient to paint the Chinese as helpless against the ruthless Japanese, so helpless and useless that a group of foreign nationals, and by foreign, I think that you mean white, that these foreigners have to rescue them?

FRANK That's not the slant I was going for—

IRENE Bad Japs rape and kill dumb Chinks. Good white people save the day. Is that more the slant you were going for?

FRANK Now come on!

AUDREY Irene!

FRANK I don't have to put up with this! You can't say that!

IRENE   You're not going to tell me what I can and cannot say!

JULIA   Irene. That's his job!

KURT   Just calm down—

IRENE   I don't care if it's his job! He's in my living room, throwing around his elitist, racist comments—

FRANK   What is your problem here really? Because I'll tell you what I think it is. It's not that you think the "foreigners," the "white people," didn't save those people in Nanking. It's because deep down you know they did. All your extensive research backs that up. And what gets you, what really gets you is that you wish it weren't true. You wish that the Chinese could've been more organized, fought back, done anything! But they didn't. They couldn't. They lay down and they were slaughtered! It was their own fault!

IRENE   What!?

KURT   That's enough! *Enough! Let's just do this!!*

IRENE   Do what?

JULIA   We have to tell you something.

KURT   I think you should sit down.

IRENE   Is there a problem?

JULIA   Well, we wanted to talk to you about the title.

IRENE   We've been over this.

JULIA   You know, compromise is a part of life. When we last were able to communicate—while you were away—we discussed the final title change.

IRENE   No, of course it's changed. The title is *Nanking: The Other Holocaust*.

FRANK   This is what we wanted to talk to you about.

IRENE   They let my original title stand? It *is The Nanking Holocaust*?

FRANK   Absolutely not.

IRENE   I'm sorry. I'm confused. My original title, *The Nanking Holocaust*, wasn't approved, right?

JULIA   Yes. There were many objections, as you know.

IRENE   I know. They didn't like the word "holocaust."

JULIA   A word with too many connotations. They felt you could appear to be trying to draw on sympathy—

IRENE   I'm not trying to take anything away from anyone.

JULIA   I know. But a perception that you were—

IRENE   I was using a word. In the proper context. If it wasn't in a title it would be "holocaust" with a small "h." Holocaust: from the Greek holos, meaning whole. Kaustos, meaning burned. Completely burned.

JULIA   It's too evocative and it was always unlikely to pass…

IRENE   But the compromise? What we decided on—

JULIA   I thought they might go for it, but y'know I had some questions myself—

IRENE   *Nanking: The Other Holocaust.* What's wrong with that?

FRANK   They liked that one even less.

IRENE   Why? That doesn't make any sense!

FRANK   The issue was primarily the "other." Its implications were that Nanking was the other—

IRENE   That's what I wanted to imply!

JULIA   But by doing so, by implying that Nanking was the "other holocaust," by default you're also implying that "The Holocaust" was the only other one in history.

FRANK   Definitely more problematic than the first.

IRENE   So—what are you saying? What are you saying? That my book has gone to print with an unknown title!

JULIA   It was going to print. And you were in the hospital. Kurt and I couldn't find Audrey…

IRENE   What is the title?

JULIA   I consulted with legal and with Kurt. He had your power of attorney. We made a decision.

IRENE   What is the title, Julia?

JULIA   We made a decision that got your book on the shelves. We made a decision that would make sure people will read about Nanking!

IRENE   *What is it!!*

    Beat.

JULIA   It's called *The Nanking Incident.*

    Bigger beat.

KURT   Irene…

AUDREY   Omigod.

IRENE   I don't know what to say. I don't. Frankly—I'm shocked. I'm shocked and hurt that you, all of you, would let this happen.

JULIA   No, wait—

IRENE   *The Nanking Incident?* It wasn't an incident. It was far, far worse and more horrible than an incident.

JULIA   I know, but let me explain our reasoning—

IRENE   There is no reasoning. There can't be any reason behind a decision like that! That title is absurd! It's ridiculous! It's not only reductive, it's revisionist!

JULIA   I want to talk about the revisionists! The people who've been harassing you, they were behind the delay…

IRENE   I gathered that.

JULIA   But this is precisely why we chose "Incident."

IRENE   Because you're playing right into their hands. You're helping them to erase history. You're aiding a denial of war crimes on a massive scale. Diminishing any culpability, any responsibility—

JULIA   No, no, no, no—

IRENE   Then what? Yes! Please explain to me!

JULIA   If I was some kind of right-wing nut, which you know very well that I'm not. But if I was, and hell-bent on Japanese nationalism, it would be much easier for me to argue against a Nanking *Holocaust* than a Nanking *Incident.* Do you see? There is too much evidence to deny an "*Incident.*" It would make those radicals seem completely irrational if they tried to do that. These groups would lose any credibility they had with moderate thinkers. Do you see? Do you see how it's a better choice?

IRENE   It's easier to build a case against a holocaust—

JULIA   Yes…

IRENE   But harder to build against an incident?

JULIA   Not harder—virtually impossible.

AUDREY   So the title… makes it more difficult for people to deny what happened.

JULIA   Exactly.

AUDREY   I see.

IRENE   I don't.

JULIA   I'm trying to help you, your book.

IRENE   Changing the title doesn't have to do with sales?

JULIA   Oh, I would never presume to say that. Never. Doesn't selling more books help you?

IRENE   Yes—but…

JULIA   Say you're browsing in a big bookstore on a Saturday afternoon? You come across a series of books, each with the title *Holocaust* and *Massacre* and *Atrocity* and lastly *Incident.* Which one of those would you pick up?

IRENE   Well…

JULIA   I know exactly which ones you'd pick up. The rest of us folk, us average types wouldn't bother with those for our weekend reading. No, we would choose *Incident.*

FRANK   It almost sounds like "innocent," doesn't it?

JULIA   *(to FRANK)* You're not helping.

AUDREY   So these average types, they'd end up reading her book. Otherwise they would've walked right by it?

JULIA   Exactly. Don't you want more people reading your book? How much of the market would you be eliminating if they don't even bother to pick the book up? That's marketing. Tricking people into doing things they don't want to do. And facing Nanking? Not many people want to do that.

IRENE   This is not my title. I will not allow it to be published this way.

FRANK   It's done. Your husband signed off on it. There's nothing you can do.

IRENE   No. I won't let it. Kurt? Say something!

AUDREY   Irene. Think about it. It's just a title!

IRENE   No! Kurt?!

KURT   Irene—Julia's right! She's right! That's why I agreed!

IRENE   Kurt!

JULIA   It would not have been published at all with "holocaust" in the title. Referring to Nanking as a holocaust is inflammatory.

FRANK   You can't compare Nanking to the Holocaust—

IRENE   The facts are here and it is indisputable. In Nanking, 1937, Japanese troops committed some of the most horrific atrocities in the history of warfare. I'm not trying to say that Nanking was more important, or that more people died, or it was the only time in the history that—

FRANK   What then?

IRENE   I'm just trying to put a spotlight on it. It's been forgotten for so long—I don't want people to forget! The numbers from Nanking are real. The Japanese army kept records, the Red Cross kept records, the journalists from all countries kept records. The established numbers—from a number of sources—during the initial six week invasion period, twenty thousand women and children raped. At least three hundred thousand dead! In six weeks! I know that three hundred thousand Chinese is not the same as six million Jews. They are not comparable—nor are they meant to be. They were individuals… men, women, children, people! This is not about victims or who has been more victimized in history! Of course, there are countless atrocities, the Turks against the Armenians, Hutus against the Tutsis, hell, the Chinese amongst themselves! I am not talking about those atrocities, I am not talking about the numbers! I am talking about Nanking, 1937. This is what I am talking about. And to dismiss Nanking—to dismiss the three hundred thousand dead, to dismiss three hundred thousand individuals—to treat them as trivial, to refer to their deaths as an "incident," well—its as bad as denial of the Holocaust.

JULIA   No one is dismissing your claims.

FRANK   It's just that Holocaust, even in your usage now, has long been associated with the Jews and the Nazis…

IRENE   Okay! Let's talk about the Jews and the Nazis.

FRANK   You just finished saying it has nothing to do with them!

IRENE   Let's talk about them, because I want to talk about them!

Yes, there was Niklas Hermann. He wrote and complained to Hitler. But there were other Germans, other Nazi members in Nanking. And when it was all over, when all the raping and pillaging had been done, they wrote reports too. They were witness to the unequivocal disastrous invasion of Nanking, the sloppiness, the heaps of bodies in the street, the killing of citizens one by one with bayonets. It was messy and time-consuming and put the average foot soldier at risk. The undisciplined nature of the invasion by Japan had such an effect that these Nazis recommended that Germany never operate this way. They condemned Japan for their inefficient and bad warfare. So— what? Better to keep citizens complacent, so they would not panic, so that foreigners would not have time or cause to react. Better, at first to cordon off the citizens in their own city. Mark them so that everyone knows who they are. Control them with walls and checkpoints, and eventually… eventually, invite them to pack a bag and take a train ride into the countryside. I believe the legacy of Nanking is that it instilled in the Nazis a need to be more efficient killers!

KURT   Let's try, let's try and talk about this rationally—

IRENE   Talk? Talk about what, Kurt? What do you want to talk about?

KURT   God. I can't even hear you! Listen to yourself!

IRENE   We are talking about my book, my work—

JULIA   Let's try and calm down, c'mon—

IRENE   My work—you're trying to deny me a voice. This is how it starts goddamit. This is how it starts. You are trying to deny me and in doing so, you're denying every person who was killed in Nanking, every woman who was systematically raped—

KURT   Stop, I can't stand it!

IRENE   And not just the Japanese in Nanking… I'm talking about all women caught in war! Rape as a weapon of war, as a part of an imperialistic plan to terrorize a population! Rape as a genocidal plan to wipe out child-bearers and ruin ethnic lines! But worse! Omigod worse than that! The refusal to acknowledge it. The systematic denial of it! That's like taking the women and raping them again!

KURT   Stop it! Shut up! Shut up!

IRENE   I know you can't acknowledge it. I know you can't! Your family has you so fucked up and turned around you can't even see straight! I know that you wish the raping of women in Nanking was a "by-product," a happenstance amidst chaos, an unfortunate consequence of war, but it was not! It was not some wishy-washy story of your grandfather on the beach stuck between two hard choices. Your grandfather had a choice. He either participated in the rapes as a loyal member of the Japanese army or he did not. My evidence says he did.

>   *Silence. Then FRANK clears his throat.*

FRANK   Irene. The book has gone to print. Your contract commits you to promoting it. I ensure that you don't get Hartford into a lawsuit. I expect you at the meeting tomorrow before the launch. I think we're done here.

>   *He starts to go.*

IRENE   Julia, please—you're not going to let this happen, are you?

JULIA   I'm not sure what you want me to say.

IRENE   I want you to say that you're not going to let this happen.

JULIA   I can't…

FRANK   It's a done deal.

IRENE   Why keep it from me? Why wait until—

JULIA   It came up, and Kurt and I discussed it…

IRENE   Why not discuss it with me?

JULIA   You were not available!

FRANK   Julia! Let's go!

IRENE   I don't believe this!

JULIA   Look! I want nothing more than to see the book's success! Do you understand? I would not have commissioned it otherwise. It's just a title, a small compromise! It will get your book on the shelves! You may hate me, you may curse my name up and down, but it doesn't change the fact that I'm on your side!

> *IRENE cannot answer. The cell phone, forgotten, rings. The room stops.*

IRENE   What should I do?

KURT   Get it if you want.

AUDREY   Maybe it's Mom?

JULIA   Someone get it.

> *It rings. Finally FRANK answers the phone.*

FRANK   Hello?… This is Frank. Who's calling?… *(to the group, handing over the receiver)* Sean? Do you know a Sean?

AUDREY   Claire's boyfriend?

FRANK   *(into the phone)* And what would this be regarding?… Hang on. *(to the group)* Wants to congratulate you on the book. *(into the phone)* Look, this isn't really the best—

> *IRENE takes the phone from him.*

IRENE   Hello, Sean? Irene. What?

> *Her tone and body language immediately shift.*
>
> *They move towards her, but she shakes her head and waves them off. They try to get the phone from her, but she is insistent on taking the call herself.*

Why would you say something like that?… Are you going to read the book?… No, I want to know. Are you going to read it?… Give me your address, I'd be happy to arrange a copy…. Look, I think if you actually read it…

> *A long extended beat as IRENE listens intensely. And then suddenly—*

Shut up! Shut the fuck up! You're perverted—you know that! You're fucking sick!

JULIA takes the phone.

JULIA   I don't know who the hell you think you are, but we've had security tracing these calls for weeks, so we'll find you, don't you fucking worry! You stupid fuck! We'll sue your ass so bad you won't even know— *(to the group)* He hung up.

KURT   Damn, damn, damn, dammit!

JULIA   Honey, are you okay?

AUDREY   Is that true? Are the calls being traced?

JULIA   No.

IRENE   Oh god.

AUDREY   What did he say?

IRENE   He said—that if I didn't stop writing about this. He'd give me what I deserve. He do to me what the soldiers did in Nanking. He'd tie me down, take a bayonet and…

She cannot finish.

JULIA   Frank—what legal recourse does she have? What can we do?

FRANK   Where's my phone?

JULIA   Should we tap her phones?

KURT   But it's an actual threat isn't it?

FRANK   Kurt! We're working on it!

JULIA   I'll call head office!

FRANK   Hello… yes… I'd like to make a report.

IRENE   Stop it.

They ignore her.

FRANK   My client has just received a very nasty call…

IRENE   I said stop it! Stop it, stop it, stop it!

She grabs FRANK's phone and throws it.

FRANK   What the hell!?

IRENE   I'm not going to go along with this! I won't!

AUDREY   Calm down!

KURT   We're trying to keep you safe!

JULIA   Irene—

IRENE   No! I don't want my phones tapped! I'm not going to live that way!

JULIA   But this threat, it is a real threat. For your protection—

IRENE   *Nooooo!* I said no! Am I making myself clear?

KURT   Irene—we're only trying to help you—

IRENE   Get out! Get out of my house!

AUDREY   Irene!

JULIA   I'm going to send security okay? I'll make sure—

IRENE   No! No security! I don't want to be guarded!

JULIA   I'm sorry—I have to. You'll thank me later.

IRENE   I'll thank you?

>   *IRENE is calm for a second and then flips out, lunging for JULIA.*

Get out! Get out of my house! *Get out!*

>   *Everyone pulls her back but she struggles.*

KURT   Hey! Hey! C'mon now. C'mon.

>   *She is held back, still yelling.*

IRENE   Get them out! Get them out!

>   *AUDREY manages to separate IRENE from JULIA.*

KURT   *(to JULIA)* Are you okay?

FRANK   You are crazy!

JULIA   I am trying to help you! Kurt, we'll talk tomorrow. I'll call you tomorrow.

>   *They exit.*

AUDREY   *(to IRENE)* Are you okay? Do you want water or something?

>   *IRENE nods. AUDREY goes.*

IRENE   Why did she say that?

KURT   What?

IRENE   That you'll "talk tomorrow"?

KURT   We will.

IRENE   No, she meant that you will. You will talk to her about me. As if I am an item to be discussed—

KURT   I didn't mean it that way—

IRENE   Why can't you support me?

KURT   What more do you want?

IRENE   I want you to support me!

KURT   How am I not doing that!? I'm coming tomorrow!

IRENE   So we'll look like a happy couple!

KURT   When you started this, I supported you. I stopped working. I helped you research, I translated. I made a choice to support you and I did everything that I could! It was hard, god it was hard. It only got harder and harder as you got more obsessed. Your head was always buried in some new research. It was always your work.

IRENE   So my work isn't important?

KURT   Now you're putting words in my mouth.

IRENE   You're my husband, you're supposed to support me.

KURT   Yes, I'm your husband, and you act like I'm barely alive! When have you ever asked me how my day was? When have you ever asked me how I'm feeling? I have to beg you to come and sit down and eat with me. I have to beg you to spend some time, any time with me! When was the last time we even kissed?

IRENE   You're the one that's distant! It's you, not me!

KURT   How am I even supposed to approach you? Most days I can't even get near you without getting my head cut off!

IRENE   You're the one that decided to sleep in the spare room!

KURT   How can I possibly sleep in our bed? I can't come to bed! You've always got piles of books and papers, all around you! You're always reading into the night. You bury yourself under the weight of those books! When I come to bed, that's all I can think about—those women and what happened to them! Those images, they float around us, girls with their legs open, women's breasts cut off…. All those pictures, they're in bed with us every night. It's horrible!

IRENE laughs bitterly.

IRENE   I don't see myself as those women who were victimized. I don't see those pictures as me. Do you see yourself as the perpetrator?

KURT   What?

IRENE   Why do you assume the part of the rapist?

KURT   How can I not? The only Japanese men in those pictures, in your book, the entire book are rapists and bloodthirsty killers!

IRENE   What?! Do you think that I think that you are a "rapist"? A "bloodthirsty killer"? What—that I'm afraid that you'll suddenly turn into a ravaging beast? What are you talking about, Kurt? What are you actually talking about it? Are you really so fucked up, that a book, my book would make you lose your manhood? That you can't get it the fuck up, because thousands of your countrymen did? Because you can't face the fact that your grandfather fucked his brains out in Nanking!!

A long beat as KURT tries to keep his composure.

KURT   You… I put up with so much. I've tried to help you, but…

Beat.

IRENE   I'm sorry. I'm sorry I said that. About your grandfather.

KURT   He was a nice man, gentle.

IRENE   He was there.

KURT   I know.

Beat.

I thought that we could fix this… but… you're too far.

And then he is gone from her life. AUDREY enters when she hears the door close.

AUDREY   Did he go?

IRENE   Yeah.

Beat. The doorbell rings. Beat.

AUDREY   I'll get it.

She goes for the door quickly.

It's your books. Help me.

IRENE and AUDREY bring the carton into the living room and open it.

They look good. They look great, Irene. They're really beautiful.

IRENE   Look at this title…. Thank you, Julia.

AUDREY   Holocaust or Incident or whatever. It doesn't matter. It's just a title. The writing, the book itself, it's yours. It's you.

A beat as they admire it.

The cover, it's beautiful. Looks like it was done in oils. Really striking.

She links arms with IRENE, something from their childhood.

Irene, if you believe in what you say, you have to trust that.

IRENE   "The Nanking Incident."

AUDREY   Your job's over. So let it go. You can't do any more.

IRENE   "By Irene Wu."

IRENE flips through wordlessly, stopping to read, and then flipping to another section. Until finally AUDREY takes it from her.

AUDREY   Here. Give it to me. Nope. You can look at it tomorrow. Why don't you go take a bath.

IRENE   I don't want to take—

AUDREY   Go. Okay?

IRENE doesn't move.

I know! I'll get your present. It's still in my car!

AUDREY starts to go.

IRENE   Audrey, why don't you have a coat?

AUDREY   Oh for god's sake! Go take a bath!

AUDREY exits. IRENE sits for a moment and goes down to her office. She is only gone a moment, then returns, perhaps carrying a towel. She crosses to the bathroom and goes inside. We hear the water running. AUDREY enters with her present, in a gift bag. It's a sort of clay statue. AUDREY sits on the floor next to the bathroom door. She takes her gift out of the bag to look at it. The water turns off.

(through the door) I can't wait to show you. I made it! It's not bad, if I do say so myself. Actually—Kurt helped. When you two were in Nanjing, I asked him to bring me back some clay from the riverbank. And I made it into this statue. Just like that Japanese general who made the statue of Kwanyin from the soil of the Yangtze mixed with mud from his garden. He was begging for mercy for his sins in Nanking. It didn't help him—he was executed anyway. Maybe it helped his spirit. Anyway, of course you don't have to beg for mercy, but Kwanyin is also for those who are suffering in their souls. So that's why I made you one. It's sorta like a modern Kwanyin. I thought, I thought, you could look at it and know that when things were bad, you could look at this statue and know that I'm here. This time, I promise, I'll be here for you. I'm here.

Silence and suddenly a single gunshot from inside the bathroom.

(as needed) Irene…. Omigod. Irene. Open up open up. Please god… open up!

AUDREY is crying, trying to get the door open. But she knows. She continues to bang and try to open the door. Perhaps she tries to call 911. She is crying hysterically now.

(as needed) Somebody help me, please, somebody, somebody, help me!

As she cries, her language shifts to Mandarin if possible. The front door opens. Unnoticed by AUDREY, who has her back to him, a man brandishing a gun enters. As he gets closer to the bathroom door, we see that he has a Nazi armband. It is NIKLAS Hermann. She finally sees him and presses herself against the bathroom door in fear for now she is no longer AUDREY, but BIG MEI.

NIKLAS   Come here.

BIG MEI shakes her head.

The soldiers have gone. We've chased them away. Is there anyone else here? Who lives here?

BIG MEI   You speak Chinese…

NIKLAS   Who lives here! Come on! I cannot help you if you do not help me!

BIG MEI   My husband…

NIKLAS   Yes… and…

BIG MEI   My husband, Lu…

NIKLAS   Anyone else…

BIG MEI   His parents… and his younger brother and sister.

NIKLAS   So five others? Five other than you?

BIG MEI   Yes.

NIKLAS   No one else?

BIG MEI   No.

> *A beat as NIKLAS registers that there is no one else left.*

NIKLAS   All right. We are going to leave here, all right? The Japs might come back.

> *She nods.*

Come here.

> *She hesitates.*

I promise, I will not hurt you.

> *He throws his coat over her and takes her under his arm.*

Now make me a promise. When we walk through the courtyard, promise me that you will look up? Do not look down. Can you do that?

BIG MEI   Why?

NIKLAS   Do it now. Look up.

> *She holds her head up.*

Do not look down. I don't want you to see…

Ella Chan
photo by Guntar Kravis

She squeezes her eyes closed.

Let's go. Let's go somewhere safe.

They exit through the door and into the past.

End of Act One.

act two

nanking – 1937

*The second act is different than the first act in that the settings
should be imagistic and simple. There should be a sense that this
act is muddier, dirtier and indeed a natural type floor covering
would add to this effect. It is more theatrical and loose, an act
that has more to do with chaos and uncontrollable elements.*

scene one

*LITTLE MEI is surrounded by a heap of bodies. Her throat has
been slit. Snow is falling, obscuring her face like tears.*

LITTLE MEI   Snow falls and I am in Nanking's wintry embrace.
The cold advances and so,
Girls I knew, women who were strangers.
Soft arms entwined, like schoolgirls on their way to class
What will happen today?

A trickle, a stench, a heaviness never to be undone
Their lives lost protect me now.

I am held in a blanket of bodies,
Piled on top of them, heaped on top of me.
Their blood, it mixes and mingles with mine
Life and deadly wounds indistinguishable.
Their rigid and torn flesh,
Absorbs the piercing eye and point of a passing soldier.
Eighteen times he walks by and I am ever silent.

Alert, their wide eyes remain on call.
There is security among their wounds.
There is safety under their open gaze.
They are my watchers and protectors,
Fallen heroes, my corpsely guards.

Grace Lynn Kung
photo by Guntar Kravis

Oozing and cast aside,
They open their arms,
And I learn the strength of their embrace.

> *The bodies close in on LITTLE MEI, who wakes up with a start
> from her nightmare.*

Ah!

scene two

> *December 15, 1937, two days after the invasion of Nanking.
> The attic of Ginling College is filled with hundreds of young
> women, trying to sleep. Dim, with a shaft of moonlight from
> a small window. LITTLE MEI, sitting up on a thin pallet,
> seemingly lying among corpses except in the quiet night,
> we hear sniffles, coughing, etc.*

LITTLE MEI pants and breathes deeply, trying to recover. Voices from the dark.

GIRL ONE   Shhhhhh!

GIRL TWO   Go to sleep!

GIRL ONE   Every damn night! Go back to sleep!

LITTLE MEI   At least I don't cry all night!

GIRL ONE   Shut up!

> *After a bit, LITTLE MEI crosses to a bucket barely lit by the shaft of light. She lifts up her skirt, squats over the bucket and starts to pee.*

It's already full!

LITTLE MEI   Well, I have to go!

GIRL TWO   It's gonna spill everywhere!

LITTLE MEI   I'm not going outside!

GIRL TWO   You're too ugly for the Japs anyway!

> *The girls cackle as LITTLE MEI finishes and returns to her pallet. She tries to sleep, but she is cold. ANNA Mallery enters, brushing off snow. She is carrying a lantern and has a pallet over her arm.*

ANNA   It's me, girls. You should take care to be quieter. We could hear you downstairs.

> *NIKLAS enters, followed by BIG MEI, still wearing his coat.*

The other attics are the same, filled to the rafters with girls.

NIKLAS   What about the regular dormitories?

ANNA   No. We've learned to empty them at night. We can't guard them, and the walls aren't high enough. The soldiers can easily scale them.

NIKLAS   And have they?

ANNA   Many times, Mr. Hermann.

NIKLAS   It's only been two days since the invasion!

ANNA   Two long days and nights, Mr. Hermann.

NIKLAS   It's freezing up here.

ANNA   We warm bricks in the ovens before bedtime.

He reaches down to touch one.

NIKLAS   This one is cool.

ANNA   They go to bed at sundown. It can't be helped.

NIKLAS   A fire, maybe?

ANNA   They'd die from the smoke. We've done all that we can.

NIKLAS   But no blankets. No beds.

ANNA   We've saved them for the sick.

BIG MEI is hit with a wave of nausea.

BIG MEI   Excuse me, but…

ANNA   *(indicating the bucket)* Over there…

LITTLE MEI   It's already full!

BIG MEI proceeds to throw up noisily as ANNA and NIKLAS exchange looks.

BIG MEI   I'm sorry…

ANNA   Here's your bed. Try to get some sleep.

NIKLAS   *(addressing LITTLE MEI)* You, can you move over?

LITTLE MEI doesn't respond.

Do you understand me? What dialect do you speak?

ANNA   She's from Shanghai.

NIKLAS   Well, that explains it. *(He winks at her.)* A city girl. Should've known. City girls are the prettiest. How is my Shanghai-*ese*? Do you understand me now?

LITTLE MEI doesn't respond to his wink, nor his switch of dialect.

ANNA   She's from an orphanage in the French Concession. [3] The
Sisters of St. Marguerite evacuated when the Japanese invaded, but
she didn't leave with them. Foolish girl, showed up at the gate weeks
after the Sisters arrived by truck. Probably walked the whole way.
Stubborn. [4]

Mei. Move over! She understands you perfectly.

> *LITTLE MEI doesn't budge.*

Mei, do as you're told!

> *LITTLE MEI moves over, which takes her directly into the shaft
> of moonlight and beside the bucket. BIG MEI starts to remove
> the coat.*

NIKLAS   You keep it. You need it to stay warm.

ANNA   That isn't necessary.

NIKLAS   My wife gave it to me, brought it all the way from her last trip
to Germany! Go on. It is the finest quality wool!

BIG MEI   Thank you.

> *She bows low, making NIKLAS uncomfortable.*

NIKLAS   It's just a coat, no need…

ANNA   Good night, girls.

NIKLAS   Good night, Mei, and…

BIG MEI   Mei. My family, they called me Big Mei…

NIKLAS   Big Mei? But—you are little?

BIG MEI   I know.

NIKLAS   *(to ANNA)* Thirty years in China and I still don't understand
their nicknames!

> *ANNA just shrugs.*

---

3 An area of Shanghai designated for French use in the Treaty of Nanking, 1862. It has
Parisian-style architecture and was infamous for its decadence and lawlessness in the
twenties and thirties, thus the appearance of Christian missionaries in the area.

4 Little Mei actually remained in Shanghai to search for her mother among the brothels,
only to learn that her mother had also been evacuated to Nanking. But that, really, is
another story.

Good night, Big Mei of Nanking. I guess that makes you Little Mei of Shanghai—good night.

ANNA and NIKLAS exit.

BIG MEI   What is this place?

LITTLE MEI   You didn't see, when you came in?

BIG MEI   I had my eyes closed.

LITTLE MEI   Why?

BIG MEI   Mr. Hermann told me to…

BIG MEI starts to heave again and leans over LITTLE MEI to reach the bucket. False alarm. She settles back on her pallet, wrapped in the coat and starts to cry. LITTLE MEI looks at her dispassionately.

I'm going to have a baby!

BIG MEI starts to cry harder.

LITTLE MEI   Don't…

BIG MEI   My husband…

She scrabbles, as if trying to crawl away.

I have to go back, I have to go back…

LITTLE MEI   Stop it!

BIG MEI cries even harder and louder. Distraught, she is finally feeling the horror she had experienced.

BIG MEI   They're all gone, they need me, my family… I have to go back!

BIG MEI starts keening incoherently. LITTLE MEI doesn't know how to react, except to grab her.

LITTLE MEI   Hey! Hey you! Stop it! Shut up, okay! Shut up!

Listen, listen to me! Do you know what I saw? I was down by the river, where it meets the city wall. Do you know what I saw up on top of the wall?

BIG MEI continues to cry.

Babies. But not normal babies. Small. Some as small as the palm of your hand. Like once, I bit into an egg, but it still had a baby chicken inside. Like that. Babies that were still meant to be inside the egg. A whole line of them, red and covered with snow. A whole army of little babies. Their little fists clenched tight.

> *She is right in BIG MEI's face with her fists.*

One baby had her fist raised in the air, as if to say, "You forgot about me! Jiu Ming *[Save my life]*! Jiu Ming *[Save my life]*! Save my life!"

BIG MEI   Why are you telling me this? Why?

LITTLE MEI   You keep crying like that and the soldiers'll find this attic and come marching up the stairs. That's what they do to Chinese babies! Is that what you want? Open your eyes.

> *LITTLE MEI turns over to try and sleep, but the moonlight is in her eyes. She resigns to laying back, eyes open.*

scene three

> *The same night. NIKLAS is walking quickly and ANNA is close behind. They are approaching the gates of Ginling College. Chaos, fire and shouting can be heard on the outside. There is a GUARD posted.*

ANNA   Now wait a minute, wait a minute, Mr. Hermann! You have no authority here! This is not your factory and it most certainly is not Germany.

NIKLAS   Tell me, Sister. If my presence, as a German national, can keep the Japanese from interfering, than you should thank God that I am here!

ANNA   It is God that I am concerned about. My conscience cannot allow me to simply hand over Ginling College!

NIKLAS   Look around! There is no Ginling. There is no Nanking. There are only the thousands of dead and those that soon will be.

> *NIKLAS yanks on the gate.*

Is it secure?

ANNA   It can be locked.

NIKLAS   It's barely nine feet high. A grown man could climb over it in minutes.

ANNA   It's designed to keep schoolgirls in, not soldiers out!

NIKLAS   It's not high enough.

ANNA   It's how high it is, Mr. Hermann! I can't change that!

NIKLAS indicates the GUARD outside the gate.

NIKLAS   And this guard?

ANNA   His name is Zhang.

NIKLAS   Can he be trusted? Can he fight?

ANNA   He was the gardener. He grew nice cabbages.

NIKLAS   But can he fight?

Suddenly the GUARD starts shouting at a passing unseen soldier.

GUARD   *(shouting in Mandarin if possible)* Hey! Don't come any closer! You hear me! Don't come any closer!

NIKLAS yanks open the gate and holds up his lantern, standing in front of the GUARD and protecting him from the unseen assailant.

NIKLAS   *(pointing to the swastika on his sleeve)* Germany, do you understand? Germany! Not Chinese! No Chinese! Now get out of here!

Roughly, NIKLAS pulls the hapless GUARD inside.

(to the guard) Keep the gates locked and stay on the grounds, or you will be dead inside a day. Do you understand?

GUARD   Yes.

NIKLAS   Do you have a gun?

GUARD   No.

NIKLAS   Go get an axe or a rake! Anything you can use as a weapon!

The GUARD hesitates, looking at ANNA.

Go!

He goes.

ANNA   Mr. Hermann. What are you doing?!

NIKLAS   Making Ginling safer. What does it look like I am doing?

ANNA   You can't— You can't march in here with orders for my staff—

NIKLAS   Your staff are ill-prepared for the onslaught. Who knows how many more soldiers will be pouring into Nanking. Those that can be armed need to be armed. See that it is done!

ANNA   Mr. Hermann!

NIKLAS   At my house, there are over one hundred women and children in the cellar. I will bring them here at dawn tomorrow.

ANNA   You cannot bring any more women here! What do you expect us to do? We don't have the room. They will have to go somewhere else!

NIKLAS   Where? Should they remain on my property? Shall I leave them undefended at my house, on grounds without gates or guards? How long can I protect them by myself?

ANNA   I have to think of my students and the Sisters! If we should open the doors to others then it's likely we'd all perish! We only have facilities for three thousand!

NIKLAS   Ginling can hold many more!

ANNA   We don't have enough resources, there's no rice, no coal!

NIKLAS   Then I will find you some. I will find it and carry it here on my back.

ANNA   The attics are overflowing. There isn't a single bed left!

NIKLAS   What about the classrooms, the chapels or even the grounds?

ANNA   They can't sleep on the ground. It's winter!

NIKLAS   I think very shortly, Sister, no one will much care where they sleep. The college is an enclosed compound with stone walls. With wells to draw water. With its own infirmary!

ANNA   How can I help you? I'm already taking care of my girls!

NIKLAS   In the name of God, there are more that need your help!

The ports are captured, the bridges flooding with troops, bands of soldiers rove the streets leaving rape and murder behind. Sister…

Since the city was taken, I have been scouring the streets! I have seen Chinaman after Chinaman carted off like so many dogs! Shot through and dumped in the Yangtze. Entire families ravished and slain, their bowels open to the air. Building after building, body after body…

When I returned to my home… what did I find at my kitchen table? Where once I sat for breakfast, Sister! What did I find, but soldiers lined up, waiting for their turn! Their trousers dragging against their ankles! The blood was not dry. And with my hands, my own hands, I pulled a monster off a wretched servant girl. She was no more than ten years old.

A refuge, Sister. A camp for the women, the weak. A sanctuary to save Nanking. While there are still some alive to be saved.

> IMAGE: A cart filled with women, defeat on their faces, or arms outstretched, Jiu Ming [Save my life]!

scene four

> Daytime, a few days later. Gardener ZHANG exits out of the gates, chasing the cart.

ZHANG (in Mandarin) Stop, stop! Let them go! I beg you, let them go!

> He is shot and seemingly dies, leaning against a wall. LITTLE MEI and BIG MEI appear out of hiding.

BIG MEI Is he dead?

LITTLE MEI He looks dead.

BIG MEI He was the gardener.

> Beat.

We shouldn't stand so close to the gate. Why did you drag me out here?

LITTLE MEI Didn't you hear them? Didn't you hear them crying?

BIG MEI Everyone could hear them!

LITTLE MEI   Maybe thirty or forty women, don't you think?

BIG MEI   I didn't look.

LITTLE MEI   I did. I wanted to see them. See them with my very own eyes. Look at every single face.

BIG MEI   Why?

>   *LITTLE MEI doesn't answer.*

What if the soldiers decided they wanted us too?

LITTLE MEI   It's all right. They've gone.

BIG MEI   Still!

LITTLE MEI   Still. If they tried, I'd fight. I'd kick. I'd scream. I'd fight them.

BIG MEI   *(indicating the corpse)* Like he did?

>   *LITTLE MEI doesn't answer.*

Maybe his family will find him. Maybe they'll find him and bury him.

LITTLE MEI   Maybe they're dead.

BIG MEI   Well, if they're not dead, they should be ashamed of themselves. They should come back for him.

LITTLE MEI   They're not coming back for him. His wife and daughter were in the cart. They're probably already dead, or wished they were…. Wait here.

>   *LITTLE MEI starts to climb over the fence.*

BIG MEI   What are you doing?

LITTLE MEI   Ssssh.

BIG MEI   What are you doing?

>   *LITTLE MEI goes up to the corpse and takes his cap. She tries to remove his shoes. They're stuck.*

Get back here! Little Mei!

>   *Giving up, LITTLE MEI tries to get his coat off, with a little more success. As she tries to work the sleeve off, suddenly the corpse moves. He reaches for her and grabs her arm hard. His mouth open, he lets out a slow, unearthly sound like*

*a demented valve. He dies, still gripping LITTLE MEI. She
extricates his hand and makes her way to the safe side of the
gate with only the cap.*

Are you okay?

LITTLE MEI   *(tucking her hair in)* Well, it's better to look like a man
isn't it?

BIG MEI looks at her in shock.

Let's just go, all right?

LITTLE MEI tries to take BIG MEI's arm, but she pulls away.

What?

BIG MEI   Don't—don't touch me.

LITTLE MEI   What? Why?

BIG MEI   Because, because, he just died… and…

LITTLE MEI   What?

BIG MEI   His spirit is looking for his family, so that he's remembered.
He'll… he'll… he will hang onto you…

LITTLE MEI   I don't believe in ghosts.

BIG MEI   Promise me you'll pray or light some incense! Pray for this
man's spirit!

LITTLE MEI   I'm not lighting incense for him!

BIG MEI   If you don't, if you don't, if he doesn't feel free, his spirit will
stay with you. Like a shadow that hangs on…. Every time you close
your eyes, in that space between what is real and what is other, his
spirit will be there… they are always there…

A moment as she stumbles into her memory.

The soldiers didn't knock. They kicked the door down and dragged
us out to the courtyard. My husband, Lu. We've only been married
a year. And his mother and father. And his little brother. We called
him Wei-Wei. And their little sister Jie. She was only twelve. Her face,
she was so surprised to see the soldiers, she dropped her brush and
spilled the ink…. She was so pretty, she was first…

scene five

LITTLE MEI is in the chapel, perhaps looking at a statue or image of Mary, cradling Jesus's body. ANNA enters, carrying pallets for sleeping.

ANNA   I haven't seen you here for any of the services. We have them every morning.

LITTLE MEI   No, I…

ANNA   I don't suppose the Sisters in Shanghai allowed you to miss service?

LITTLE MEI   No.

ANNA   Well, would you like to pray together? We can do our prayers in French, if you like?

LITTLE MEI   No, please.

ANNA   Well… then, I will leave you to it. Savour the solitude for now. There'll be people sleeping here tonight.

Sister ANNA turns to go, leaving the pallets.

LITTLE MEI   Sister Anna, wait. So many people have died. They're dying every day. And you help them? You're with them when they die?

ANNA   I try to be, yes.

LITTLE MEI   Even though they're dead, what happens? I mean, are they still with you?

ANNA   In a way, they will always be a part of me, yes.

LITTLE MEI   So… Sister Catherine, and Big Ears Chen, and Gardener Zhang…?

ANNA   I hold them in my heart, yes.

LITTLE MEI   How?

Instead of answering, ANNA kneels.

ANNA   That's not a question for me. Come.

LITTLE MEI does not kneel. ANNA does not pray but looks directly at LITTLE MEI.

I know that you are going outside of the gates, Little Mei. One of the nurses saw you, heading towards the river. This will not do.

LITTLE MEI is silent, resistant.

What is wrong with you? Why—why do you do it? You know how treacherous it is! Why take that chance?

LITTLE MEI   I don't know.

ANNA   You don't know? Why are you going to the river?

LITTLE MEI   It's where they dump the bodies.

ANNA   What is it you want? Tell me, so that I can help you. Let me help you. What are you looking for?

A quick and ghostly light up on...

IMAGE: A young Chinese woman on the floor scrubbing, scrubbing endlessly.

LITTLE MEI   *(with much difficulty)* I don't know.

ANNA   You're going to get yourself killed!

LITTLE MEI   Maybe that's better! Maybe it's better to be dead!

Suddenly, ANNA slaps LITTLE MEI hard across the cheek.

ANNA   Do not wish your life away so easily! You're lucky to be alive! Pray! And beg for God's forgiveness.

LITTLE MEI is in shock from the blow, looking at ANNA.

Child. I'm sorry...

Sister ANNA tries to embrace her, but LITTLE MEI pushes her out of the way and exits.

scene six

Not a realistic space, but each character in their own reality.

ANNA   Dear Lord,

Give me strength so that I may pass it on. These young women, they've lost their families, their homes.... They've lost their will, my

Lord. We found another girl in the well this morning. Another girl who will never learn the Glory of God.

How can I help them? How can I help them to believe?

LITTLE MEI   I believed my mother, when she told me, "Shh. Go to sleep, Mei-Mei. I'll be back in the morning."

BIG MEI   Kwanyin, Goddess of Mercy,

I ran and I hid, but I heard everything…. I know that the spirits of my family are in the deepest of pain. They are suffering. They refuse to rest. They are calling on me to give them peace. Can you help them, Kwanyin? Can you give them peace?

LITTLE MEI   I believe in the road along the river and my strong feet which carried me, when I felt the squish and squelch of who knows underfoot.

NIKLAS   My darling wife, you cannot imagine the horror. The city in which we loved, the city in which our children were born. You would not recognize it. Everything of value is burned or taken by force. The clocks on the walls, dried fish from the stores, and the people…. So many people.

Take care of our children. Tell them that they cannot know me, unless they see what I have seen. My sons, I will write it down for you, my sons, I will write it all down.

LITTLE MEI   I believe, throughout this wretched city, the weeping river is groaning with the bloated.

ANNA   Father, please deliver us from the plague that infects Nanking. To see the crumble, the bodies rotting in the ditch, flesh falling off faces… how many rapes? How many? Jiu Ming *[Save my life]*, they cry! Jiu Ming *[Save my life]*! Save my life!

The sound of a telegraph.

NIKLAS   Mein Führer. Stop. Important matter to discuss with you. Stop. Please contact me immediately. Stop. Regards Niklas Hermann.

ALL   Stop.

ANNA   We must not lose our faith.

scene seven

The campgrounds. NIKLAS is attaching his hand-lettered sign over the official sign that reads "GINLING COLLEGE FOR GIRLS." ANNA, LITTLE MEI and BIG MEI enter, carrying laundry. BIG MEI is wearing the coat. They stop to read the sign.

LITTLE MEI   Nanking Safety Zone
Hours of bombing: 9 am – 9 pm
Resumes: 9 pm – 9 am

ANNA   Is this a joke?

LITTLE MEI   Complaints Department Closed
Please contact the Japanese Army.

NIKLAS   A little joke.

He is met with silence.

A bit of fun. We all deserve a little smile. Now that it looks like the Safety Zone will be recognized.

ANNA   So your meeting with the diplomat went well.

NIKLAS   Yes, Fukuyama from the Embassy seemed agreeable, as far I could tell. Yes, we discussed the entirety of the Safety Zone, with Ginling reserved for women and children. Yes.

The sound of a truck at the gate.

LITTLE MEI   The supply truck!

NIKLAS   Perhaps the Japanese Embassy will bestow some treats on us!

ANNA   Not likely.

NIKLAS   Who knows? Miracles do happen.

LITTLE MEI   Hopefully there's something else besides rice…

BIG MEI   Rice porridge day after day!

ANNA   Yes. Well. Take your complaint to the Japanese.

NIKLAS   Sister, is that a joke?

ANNA   A little one.

NIKLAS   Very little, I would say.

> *LITTLE MEI stops suddenly, listening.*

LITTLE MEI   What is that?

BIG MEI   What?

LITTLE MEI   It's chickens!

BIG MEI   What!

LITTLE MEI   Chickens! Chickens! Chickens!

NIKLAS   They must be from the embassy!

ANNA   They have chickens, and day after day they only give us rice!

BIG MEI   Chickens!

ANNA   Mr. Hermann, we must try and get a few chickens if we can! Imagine, some nice soup or fresh eggs. It would do us a world of good.

NIKLAS   Well, then. Let us go and greet the chickens! Bok-bok, girls!

> *ANNA and NIKLAS exit.*

BIG MEI   I'm so hungry!

LITTLE MEI   When was the last time you had meat?

BIG MEI   I can't even remember!

LITTLE MEI   Wouldn't you like some chicken feet right now? Or roasted, with crispy salty skin!

BIG MEI   Yesterday, I didn't make it to the commissary in time and they ran out of rice! There's so many people now.

LITTLE MEI   I heard ten thousand. There's no room anywhere, that's why people are sleeping on the grounds.

BIG MEI   At least they get to have a fire.

LITTLE MEI   I guess. But some have to sleep next to the walls. Do you know what they call that when the Sisters aren't around? They call it the "lottery." Because who knows? Your chances aren't very good.

BIG MEI   Mei!

LITTLE MEI   It's true!

NIKLAS and ANNA enter with HIRO Fukuyama,
a Japanese diplomat. His fine clothing and clean hands
are quite a contrast to their appearance.

ANNA *(warning)* Girls!

Seeing HIRO, LITTLE MEI and BIG MEI stop and bow
their heads.

HIRO Ah, so this is Ginling. This is where you would like the headquarters of your "Safety Zone."

NIKLAS Yes. My apologies, Mr. Fukuyama—if we had known the Embassy was coming…. We would have prepared…

HIRO I see.

NIKLAS We are honoured that the Embassy of Japan has granted us permission to establish a Safety Zone.

HIRO Ah. So. You must understand it is not under my consideration. I speak for the Imperial word of Emperor Hirohito, whose word is absolute. This visit, my report, as well as that of the Lieutenant-General, will inform his final decision.

NIKLAS Lieutenant-General?

HIRO *(looking off to where the army is assembled)* Of the Imperial Army of Japan, Mr. Hermann.

NIKLAS I understand—we are honoured just the same.

NIKLAS and ANNA give slight bows in their direction.

ANNA What does it mean? That we must continue to wait for word from Japan—

HIRO Exactly that. So.

A beat as HIRO turns his attention to the girls. He
scrutinizes them.

They are very young.

NIKLAS Yes…

ANNA Girls. Why don't you run along? *(as they pick up the laundry)* Just leave the laundry. Leave it for later. Go. Go.

They exit.

HIRO   How many are you hosting here, Sister Mallery?

ANNA   We haven't finished registering everyone. It takes time.

HIRO   How many do you think?

ANNA   At present, I think close to seven thousand. I'm not really sure.

HIRO   Seven thousand? How many were your students, your staff?

ANNA   Again, I'm not sure. I was just a teacher before. Probably three thousand or so.

HIRO   So, the rest… *civilians*?

ANNA   Yes, women, children with no place to go.

HIRO   There are men here also, no?

ANNA   Yes, but not very many. Members of the staff, men, who work as, as, as cooks, as drivers, gardeners… ah… labourers also! And… men who recently found the Christian faith! There are men on the grounds of Ginling. That's quite normal…

HIRO   I see.

>   *A moment.*

Sister Mallery. As a part of our reports, the Imperial Army requires a visual inspection. We need to see them all.

ANNA   See them all?

HIRO   Everyone. Everyone that you are hosting here in your "Safety Zone" for civilians. Is that not clear?

NIKLAS   Yes. Absolutely. Indeed.

HIRO   Have them assemble.

NIKLAS   Of course. Of course.

ANNA   Mei. Mei! Little Mei!

>   *She re-enters.*

LITTLE MEI   Yes, Sister?

ANNA   Venez-ici! Regardez-moi. Ne le regardez pas. Regardez-moi et parlez seulement en français, d'accord? *[Come here! Look at me. Don't look at him. Look at me. Speak only in French, okay?]*

LITTLE MEI   Mais—pourquoi? *[But—why?]*

ANNA   Avertissez les soldats. Dites-leur de se cacher dans les greniers. Vous-comprenez? *[Warn the soldiers. Tell them to hide in the attics. Do you understand?]*

LITTLE MEI   Oui. *[Yes.]*

ANNA   Allez. Allez, vite! *[Go, now, hurry! Go!]*

LITTLE MEI goes.

HIRO   What did you say to her?

ANNA   Only that she should instruct everyone to assemble.

HIRO   But not in Chinese. It was French you were speaking?

ANNA   Just because the city has been invaded, doesn't mean I can't keep up with their lessons. Unless Hirohito has a problem with that.

HIRO   No indeed. *Emperor* Hirohito is keen on language studies. In fact, in my first posting, up north, in Manchukuo,[5] there were a great many foreigners also. I came to know them well. I would watch them. I would listen to them carefully. It was my job to interpret their actions, their motives. I was very good at my job.

Beat.

NIKLAS   Yes, clearly your English is excellent.

HIRO   Then I am making myself clear. Any treachery will be punished by death. Japan has no tolerance for foreign nations interfering in Japan's affairs.

NIKLAS   We understand.

HIRO looks at NIKLAS and ANNA with a fierce scrutiny.

HIRO   No tolerance. *(to NIKLAS)* Not for countries with which Japan has diplomatic relations... *(turning to ANNA)* but especially not for countries with which Japan is not currently... friendly.

Good. Shall we begin the inspection?

---

5 Manchuria is an area of northern China invaded by the Japanese in 1932 and renamed Manchukuo. Japan quickly established it as a colony with a puppet Chinese leader, Pu-Yi (also known as the "Last Emperor.") Among the few countries to officially recognize Manchukuo: Germany under Hitler and Spain under Franco. It was invaded and the government dissolved it at the end of World War II.

NIKLAS   Of course.

ANNA   Perhaps you would like to see the infirmary first...

> *HIRO looks around, as if searching for something. He spots the hand-lettered sign.*

HIRO   What is the meaning of this?

> *Nobody answers or looks.*

What. Is. *This?*

NIKLAS   Nothing.

HIRO   Is this a *joke!?*

NIKLAS   Ah. Perhaps. Just a little joke.

> *HIRO explodes, a bit forced but still with an alarming fury.*

HIRO   How dare you mock the Imperial Army of Japan! How dare you!

> *He tears the sign down and throws the pieces in their faces. NIKLAS and ANNA quickly kneel before him, heads bowed.*

Ginling will suffer at your hands! You will receive no shipments of food or coal for three days! Perhaps, after three days of hunger and cold, you'll take your position a little more seriously! This will go into my report!

> *He exits in a huff.*

(*offstage, in Japanese if possible*) Leave it, we're going! Let's go!

> *The sound of the truck driving off, into silence. Long pause.*

NIKLAS   I guess he's not doing an inspection.

> *LITTLE MEI returns out of breath.*

LITTLE MEI   Soeur Anna! Je l'ai fait! Les soldats—où est-il allé? [*Sister Anna! I did it! The soldiers—where did he go?*]

NIKLAS   It's all right, he's gone.

LITTLE MEI   What happened?

NIKLAS   My little joke distracted him!

ANNA   Yes, but at what cost, Niklas! You've put the college at risk!

NIKLAS   They won't find them now.

ANNA   It is too dangerous to hide the Chinese soldiers!

NIKLAS   They gave up their arms. They are no more soldiers than we are. They need refuge too.

ANNA   *(to LITTLE MEI)* Where are they now? In the attics?

LITTLE MEI   Yes, like you told me…

ANNA   Good. Little Mei, go and see if any of them still have their uniforms. These have to be destroyed. Do you understand?

LITTLE MEI   Yes.

ANNA   Get some of the others to help you. Go.

    She exits.

Fukuyama brought the army. If they come again, what then?

NIKLAS   Then—we will have to stay ahead of them.

ANNA   No rice, no coal. No chickens.

NIKLAS   No. Come—let us have a look at our stores and see what we can do.

scene eight

    The grounds of Ginling. LITTLE MEI is wearing NIKLAS's coat. BIG MEI is quite upset.

BIG MEI   Give it to me! Give it to me!

LITTLE MEI   You left it there!

BIG MEI   I didn't want it to get wet!

LITTLE MEI   So you should've been watching it!

BIG MEI   Give it back! I don't have anything else!

LITTLE MEI   So—that makes you special? So you deserve to be warm and I don't?

BIG MEI   But I'm—

LITTLE MEI   Everyone in Ginling has a story. Yours isn't any different.

BIG MEI   It's mine! Mr. Hermann gave it to me!

LITTLE MEI   He felt sorry for you! Because you're pathetic! Hiding like a dog in the outhouse! While your family got slaughtered!

BIG MEI   And what would you have done?

LITTLE MEI   If my family was in danger? I would've stood with them! I would've ripped flesh in my bare hands! I wouldn't have run away and let my family die!

> *BIG MEI is really stung by the comment and goes after LITTLE MEI. A tussle.*

BIG MEI   Shut up! Shut up! Give me my coat! You give it to me!

LITTLE MEI   What do you think, because Mr. Hermann gave you this coat… that what? What? There are thousands of girls in this camp! He probably doesn't even remember your name!

> *NIKLAS enters.*

NIKLAS   Girls, girls, come on. We have a surprise!

BIG MEI   Mr. Hermann.

NIKLAS   Yes.

BIG MEI   Mr. Hermann, what's my name?

LITTLE MEI   Yes. What's my name?

NIKLAS   Why, Mei, of course, you are both called Mei. Why do you ask?

BIG MEI   No reason.

NIKLAS   No, of course. *(to BIG MEI)* You are Mei of Shanghai… *(to LITTLE MEI)* and you are Mei of Nanking.

LITTLE MEI   I'm Mei from Shanghai.

NIKLAS   Oh, yes, sorry. Of course you are! The coat…. *(to BIG MEI)* You gave her the coat…

> *No answer.*

Come on, why don't we go inside?

BIG MEI   What are we doing?

NIKLAS   You will see.

LITTLE MEI What's going on?

NIKLAS They are waiting for us.

scene nine

Dining hall of Ginling. Bustle of candles and activity. Christmas Eve.

ANNA Hurry up. You girls are late.

Addressing the assembled, a large portion of the camp.

Thank you for coming. We have invited all of you to dinner, because you have made contributions to life in the camp. Whether you chose to guard the wells, or helped in the nursery, it is you who have made a refuge possible. Our meal tonight will be followed by service. We should all remember the significance of this time of year. The birth of Christ should bring us hope. Tonight we celebrate those who have given us hope, no matter how small.

NIKLAS Tonight, we have a wonderful repast! Your choice of entrée this Christmas Eve, rice, boiled on a plate. Or rice porridge in a bowl. Or dry, uncooked rice, if you prefer. As an accoutrement, there is a small quantity of salt and a sprinkling of weevils, with a touch of dirt. Enjoy! Please join the queue.

They get in line for the food, except for LITTLE MEI. ANNA approaches her.

ANNA Aren't you going to eat?

LITTLE MEI I don't want to.

ANNA You need to eat. You need to stay strong.

LITTLE MEI I don't care.

ANNA Little Mei. I'm sorry that I hit you the other day. It was a moment of weakness. There are many times when I think that I don't have the strength. It's easy to lose hope. But that is why we must fight, we must try, with all our being. We must try.

When I asked you to warn the soldiers? You were in great danger, but you didn't hesitate for a moment. You were very brave. Not many have your strength. It is your strength that will save us all. Hang onto it as long as you can, Little Mei, hang on. You might see a day when war will be no more. God speed that day.

LITTLE MEI   God speed the day.

ANNA   Amen. Come, Little Mei, please, share in the food. It's for you.

LITTLE MEI does. If possible, ANNA crosses to a piano and starts tinkling a little. BIG MEI is in line for food near NIKLAS.

BIG MEI   Mr. Hermann, do you have children?

NIKLAS   You mean, besides all of you?

BIG MEI   Yes, besides all of us…

NIKLAS   Three boys.

BIG MEI   And they're safe?

NIKLAS   Yes. Up north. With their mother in Peking.

BIG MEI   Why didn't you go with them? Where it's safe? Why are you here?

NIKLAS cannot answer, but just places his hand lightly on BIG MEI's head, looking at her with mixed emotions.

NIKLAS   I was worried about my servants and my workers. I could not leave them to die. So I stayed. For them, for Little Mei… for you.

Sister ANNA moves off to the piano and begins to sing "O Holy Night".

ANNA   O holy night! The stars are brightly shining,
It is the night of our dear Savior's birth. *(continuing under)*

NIKLAS   I'm German, but I don't know what that means anymore.

ANNA   *(softly under)* Long lay the world in sin and error pining,

NIKLAS   I'm here. This is where I belong. I am Chinese.

ANNA   *(softly under)* Till He appear'd and the soul felt its worth.

NIKLAS   You gave Little Mei the coat. That's very kind of you.

ANNA   *(softly under)* A thrill of hope the weary world rejoices,

BIG MEI   Yes…

ANNA   (*softly under*) For yonder breaks a new and glorious morn.

NIKLAS   She seems cold, but she needs our compassion.

> *BIG MEI crosses and sits down next to LITTLE MEI, still wearing the coat. During the rest of the song, BIG MEI takes her arm and rests her head on LITTLE MEI's shoulder. LITTLE MEI doesn't resist. They sit together, small.*

ANNA   Fall on your knees! O, hear the angel voices!
O night divine, O night when Christ was born;
O night divine, O night! O holy night!

> *Suddenly, a shrill siren breaks the mood. They race outside.*

Planes.

NIKLAS   There!

LITTLE MEI   They're coming fast!

ANNA   Can you see—Japanese or Chinese?

NIKLAS   Coming from the south, must be Japanese!

> *The siren changes from warning to urgent.*

ANNA   Here they come!

LITTLE MEI   They're dropping something.

BIG MEI   What is it?

NIKLAS   It's not bombs!

ANNA   Oh no!

NIKLAS   Cover your nose and mouth!

ANNA   Oh God, go inside! Go!

> *The girls run off as a rush of planes and paper fall from the sky. Leaflets trickle down like snow or ash. The siren continues underneath.*

NIKLAS   A message. From Japan.

ANNA   What does it say?

> *HIRO appears.*

HIRO   "The city of Nanking and its citizens are now officially under the rule of his Imperial Excellency, Emperor Hirohito of Japan.

All citizens must register with the Japanese army. Upon registration, each household will be given a sack of rice. Any enemy soldiers will be imprisoned and treated fairly. Only registrations with the Japanese army will be considered valid."

HIRO bows his head and the lights go out on him.

NIKLAS   Unbelievable, the nerve!

ANNA   They are making them register all over again!

NIKLAS   No, that isn't it at all. They want the "rats" to come out of hiding.

scene ten

Sister ANNA spots someone in the distance.

ANNA   Mr. Fukuyama! Oh no…

She hurries off to warn the girls.

scene eleven

In the attic. LITTLE MEI and BIG MEI are looking out the window.

LITTLE MEI   Why are we still up here! The Japanese must be gone by now.

BIG MEI   Sister Anna said to stay hidden!

LITTLE MEI   I hate waiting.

A beat.

My mother, she used to work for the Sisters. As a child, she'd stick me in a wooden bucket for hours while she cleaned the floors. I'd watch her, waiting, as she scrubbed on her hands and knees…

BIG MEI   Where is she now?

Grace Lynn Kung and Ella Chan
photo by Guntar Kravis

LITTLE MEI   I don't know. One night when I was still small, I heard
shouting. My mother and the Sisters. Arguing, because my mother
was out all night. I heard the front door slam and she was gone.
I thought, sometimes, I saw glimpses of her on the street in Shanghai.
One time, I called out and she turned around… it was her, but, but
someone pulled her away. Another time, I thought I heard her voice
in the front hallway. When I asked the Sisters, they said I was hearing
things. But then, the next day they gave me new shoes and a ribbon
for my hair…. Where did these things come from? Oh Mei, if she is
out there—how will she ever find me here in Ginling?

>   *Suddenly cries of Jiu Ming* [Save my life]*! from the courtyard.*

BIG MEI   What's going on?

LITTLE MEI   It's the man from the embassy. He's still here!

BIG MEI   And girls?! Why are there girls down there?

LITTLE MEI   Oh no! They're heading towards the gate.

BIG MEI   Oh Kwanyin, save their souls…

LITTLE MEI   How many? How many girls?

> *A large crash on the grounds.*

scene twelve

> *ANNA counts slowly, facing the audience, growing increasingly*
> *despondent. The dialogue is recent memory. Christmas Day.*

ANNA   One.

HIRO   You deluge my staff with paperwork; pleas to protect your
young women, petitions for more access to coal, reports on incidents.

ANNA   You can't help us if you don't know what we need.

HIRO   Ah. Need. Yes. I would like to propose an agreement. In the
spirit of "need."

NIKLAS   What kind of agreement?

ANNA   Two.

HIRO   Japan has taken Nanking. And with our occupation, a great
many soldiers will be stationed here. The Embassy fears that with the
rise of the number of soldiers…. The Embassy very much wants to
alleviate the number of "incidents."

NIKLAS   Incidents?

HIRO   Incidents regarding the women.

ANNA   Three.

HIRO   The army, the soldiers, require… recreation… release.

NIKLAS   No, no absolutely not. Get out.

ANNA   Let him finish.

HIRO   There are many girls here. Many you have yet to register. Is
there the possibility there that there are "professionals" who have
escaped notice?

ANNA   Four.

HIRO   Twenty girls. Of course, we could also do this without your co-operation. But perhaps, it would be… messier.

NIKLAS   No, no. This is outrageous, to be even considering it…

ANNA   Five.

HIRO   We are only seeking twenty working girls, Mr. Hermann. Provide us with the twenty girls and the Embassy will assure that Ginling will be protected from raids.

NIKLAS   We won't do this! We will not hand over young women to be in your brothel!

ANNA   Six.

NIKLAS   Anna! Consider!

ANNA   *(to NIKLAS, low)* How much longer can we keep it up? How much longer can we go without sleep trying to guard the grounds? If we guarantee that there will be no more raids? Twenty girls! There are over twelve thousand people in the camp…. If I can save them—

NIKLAS   Anna, you are talking about slavery—

ANNA   Seven.

HIRO   Your decision?

ANNA   Mr. Fukuyama, can you ensure the safety of Ginling?

HIRO   I swear by my name and my ancestors. All measures possible—

NIKLAS   All measures possible—what does that mean?

HIRO   Exactly that, Mr. Hermann.

ANNA   Eight.

NIKLAS   Anna! Do not trust him! God knows what he's thinking. How will you live with yourself?

ANNA   Content, Mr. Hermann. Content, that over twelve thousand will be safe.

NIKLAS   And what of the twenty? You cannot do this monstrous thing! I will not have any part in this! I won't!

    He exits.

ANNA   Nine.

HIRO   You will ask for volunteers. Perhaps, women who are willing, girls who… worked… in the past.

ANNA   What if there are no volunteers?

HIRO   Then you will have to choose.

ANNA   Me?

HIRO   Would you prefer I did it?

ANNA   Ten.

HIRO   You won't regret this. Japan will look kindly on your co-operation in this matter, and as I assured you, Ginling will be protected. You should instruct the women to assemble. It is best to conduct this in a timely fashion.

> *ANNA finishes counting out the rest of the girls.*

ANNA   *(with increasing difficulty)* Eleven… twelve… thirteen… fourteen… fifteen… sixteen… seventeen… eighteen… nineteen… twenty.

scene thirteen

> *NIKLAS flies in on HIRO and ANNA, heading straight for HIRO's throat.*

NIKLAS   I'll kill you with my bare hands!

ANNA   What's happened!

> *NIKLAS strikes him, viciously across the face.*

NIKLAS   A trick!

> *Again.*

A diversion! I'll kill you! The attics are empty! Empty!

> *He hits him again. HIRO staggers back.*

ANNA   What!

NIKLAS   They took them… they're gone! While you were entertaining this monster—while he was distracting us—a truck smashed through the east wall! And emptied the attics!

HIRO   No...

ANNA   How many girls?

NIKLAS   At least a hundred!

HIRO   I assure you, I knew nothing of this!

> *NIKLAS viciously attacks him, his rage from the weeks in the Safety Zone unleashed on the diplomat, in blow after blow.*

NIKLAS   You treacherous—

HIRO   *(in Japanese)* Stop it! I didn't do it. Stop! Please! I beg you!

> *HIRO collapses on the floor. NIKLAS takes out his gun and points it at him.*

NIKLAS   What have you done? I love this city. I love Nanking.

ANNA   Niklas!

> *He hesitates and drops his arm. HIRO takes his cue and makes a hasty retreat.*

Oh God!

NIKLAS   God is not here.

scene fourteen

> *Dim. Comfort Station. A room with no light and one door. LITTLE MEI is lying down. BIG MEI is thrown in. She is injured and leans against a wall for support.*

LITTLE MEI   Mei...

BIG MEI   They didn't want me, because I'm having a baby. The soldiers don't want to lie with a pregnant woman.

LITTLE MEI   That's good—isn't it?

BIG MEI   Mei... they tried to take the baby...

> *BIG MEI collapses. LITTLE MEI rushes over.*

LITTLE MEI   What...

BIG MEI   They said that there'll be no more Chinese babies… how can that be?

LITTLE MEI   You're okay, you're okay.

BIG MEI   But I can feel it, I can feel it…. Is it blood? Am I having the baby?

LITTLE MEI   No, no, no, no, no, no.

BIG MEI   Is this blood…?

LITTLE MEI   It's nothing, it's sand. It's nothing.

BIG MEI   But it's wet, it's really very wet…

LITTLE MEI   The dirt is wet… it's nothing…

BIG MEI   There's a lot of it…. It's not blood?

LITTLE MEI   No…

> *LITTLE MEI takes the coat and bundles it, pressing it into BIG MEI's abdomen, trying to stop the blood.*

Come on. Here, hold this. Come on, hold this. Put your hands here.

BIG MEI   I'm holding it. I'm holding on.

LITTLE MEI   Good. Good. Just hold onto this.

> *BIG MEI is bleeding out. A sudden sharp pain.*

BIG MEI   Will you pray for me? There's no one left to pray for me. Will you help me? If you don't, my spirit…. Promise me, that you'll remember me? Promise, you'll never forget.

LITTLE MEI   I promise.

> *BIG MEI dies.*

scene fifteen

> *Very dim. The Japanese SOLDIER enters, perhaps inebriated. He initially speaks Japanese to her. LITTLE MEI doesn't speak for the entire scene. He gestures to her.*

SOLDIER   *(in Japanese)* Get up!

He takes the coat off of BIG MEI and tries it on.

Do you understand me? It doesn't matter.

He runs his hands along her body.

You are not so cold like the others.

Did you see the river on fire today?
It's water! How can water burn?
"How can a river burn? When it's filled with bodies!"
We told that joke all day.

He grabs her and holds her close.

We set the river on fire.
It's dirty. It has to be done.
Your river is filled with filth, so it must be purified.
I can make it run clean...
China will be pure again.

Suddenly he takes out a knife and slits her throat shallowly.

Just in case you cry.

He rips her dress and starts undoing his belt.

scene sixteen

NIKLAS   Mein Führer,

ANNA   My Lord,

NIKLAS   I write to you in my position as the highest ranking Nazi official stationed in China.

ANNA   I hardly know how to ask for your guidance.

NIKLAS   It has been two weeks since the Japanese have invaded Nanking.

ANNA   Each day is like a year. I age with each death, each rape, each girl under my care. It was a grave mistake to have all the women in one place.

NIKLAS   I have documented my eyewitness accounts in the following report. The figures are from my personal diary and, I assure you, are no exaggeration.

ANNA   The devil has poisoned thought and reason in this dark place. No one but You should decide who lives or dies. I thought that I could play at being God, and now hundreds are suffering from my arrogance.

NIKLAS   Herr Hitler, I implore you. In the name of humanity, use your influence with Japan and stop this horror. To do nothing, to say nothing, to condone the wholesale slaughter of civilians and persecution of a people would be our darkest hour.

ANNA   Dear Lord, I do not ask for your forgiveness, for I do not deserve it. I do not fear hell, for I have witnessed Nanking.

scene seventeen

The courtyard.

NIKLAS   What is this? An entire delegation?

ANNA   Did Fukuyama notify you?

NIKLAS   No.

ANNA   They're coming for us.

NIKLAS   If anything is to happen, let them take me. It was my hand.

As HIRO arrives, we see some bruising on his face and maybe a bandage.

(steeling himself) Mr. Fukuyama.

HIRO   Mr. Hermann. Sister.

A beat.

I have brought visitors. Dignitaries. My superiors from Japan.

ANNA   I see. Your superiors?

HIRO   Indeed. If you'll excuse my appearance. There was an… accident.

NIKLAS   Indeed.

At that point, ANNA bows low and NIKLAS follows her lead, making a bit of a display.

HIRO hands them a piece of paper.

HIRO   Congratulations. Japan recognizes the Safety Zone. I have the word of the Emperor that the women of Ginling will no longer be harassed. As compensation for the previous incident, the Japanese government would like to provide you with one hundred sacks of rice and other rations.

NIKLAS   Compensation?

HIRO   Yes. So.

NIKLAS   One hundred sacks of rice.

Beat.

ANNA   What rations, Mr. Fukuyama?

HIRO   There is flour, salt and soybeans to be delivered today by truck.

ANNA   No meat? Some of the young women, they are with child. They need meat.

HIRO   Perhaps we can procure some dried fish, but not for today.

NIKLAS   When then? Where's the fish?

HIRO   It will arrive on our boats next week. You will accept?

ANNA and NIKLAS nod mutely.

Then our visit is concluded.

He turns to go, but stops, pulling out a book from his jacket.

Forgive me, Sister Mallery, I forgot to return this.

ANNA   Return? I don't understand.

HIRO   Your French textbook. I'm afraid I don't have enough time to continue my language studies. *(in a lower voice)* Il y a des soldats Japonais qui sont très mauvais. *[There are Japanese soldiers who are very bad.]*

ANNA   Pardon?

HIRO   J'ai moi mêmes des jeunes filles. *[I have young daughters of my own.]*

ANNA   I see. Yes. Yes, I see.

She takes the book.

If I may, your French is… quite good. Perhaps in the future, we could converse more…

HIRO   Perhaps. Good day.

He exits quickly.

NIKLAS   What did he say? Something about… daughters?

ANNA   *(opening the book)* Yes… he has daughters…. Look here, he's drawn a map.

NIKLAS   If this is the river, then this must be Ginling. And that looks like the bridge at Hanchuang.

ANNA   Ils sont ici. Les cadavres. *[They are here. The bodies.]*

NIKLAS   They are here. The bodies.

IMAGE: The heap of bodies with LITTLE MEI in the centre. They move in on her, crushing, or hugging her, until somehow she emerges physically, rising from the heap.

scene eighteen

Snow is falling.

ANNA   Here, over here. Oh my God… there are so many…

NIKLAS   The bodies are cold.

ANNA   Oh, poor souls…

Finding LITTLE MEI.

NIKLAS   Mei! It's Little Mei. Help me.

They extricate her.

ANNA   Oh dear…

NIKLAS   They slit her throat…

ANNA   Oh, my poor child…

ANNA touches her face gently.

NIKLAS   She's warm, her cheek is hot!

ANNA   She's alive!

NIKLAS   Mei! Little Mei! Wake up. Open your eyes. C'mon!

> *LITTLE MEI opens her eyes and tries to speak.*

LITTLE MEI   I promise…

> *BIG MEI appears in a ghostly glow.*

BIG MEI   Mei, born in a village on the river Qinhua
Married at age fifteen
Widowed at age sixteen
Date of death, December 26, 1937
Japanese Comfort Station, Nanking
Death by bayonet, disembowelment, loss of blood
No children, no surviving family, no future.

> *BIG MEI exits.*

> *ANNA takes LITTLE MEI into her lap, as if cradling a small child, echoing Mary holding Jesus's body if possible. LITTLE MEI weeps into ANNA's embrace.*

ANNA   I'm sorry, child, I'm sorry. It's over. It's over.

> *The snow stops and the sun comes out.*

scene nineteen

> *LITTLE MEI is writing a letter.*

LITTLE MEI   Dear Niklas,

Thank you for your letter. I am sorry to hear about the passing of your wife. With the war over, the Americans have finally arrived but I imagine that the Sisters will continue to run the camp as long as they are needed.

I work in the nursery now. There are many newborns left at the gate. It is likely their fathers are Japanese. We try to give them names of hope but there are so many, we easily run out. There are some we named Niklas and of course many more called Anna.

ANNA   Anna Mallery
Born 1886, Michigan, USA
Missionary, teacher and a servant of God
Lived and loved China for twenty-four years
Returned to America, suffering a nervous breakdown
Died 1941, released from this world by her own hand
A soldier of mercy and a casualty of war
Her gravestone reads, "Ginling Forever."

ANNA exits.

LITTLE MEI   My neck has healed, but still gives me trouble. I must practise speaking before I forget that I have a voice. Much was taken from me, but I did not lose my head. That is a little joke.

When the people here heard of your plight, they wanted to help you. We called you "Living Buddha" and Buddha must not go hungry. Here enclosed are dried fish, flour, soybeans and rice. There is also money, as much as we could collect around camp. We will continue to send these to you as long as you need and as long as we are able.

NIKLAS   Niklas Hermann,
Born Hamburg, Germany, 1882
Engineer, businessman, member of the Nazi Party
Married, and raised his family in China for thirty years
Returned to Germany with evidence of the massacre
Solicited an audience with Adolf Hitler
Arrested by the Gestapo
Released and lived the remainder of his life impoverished,
reviled, a pariah and an outcast.

Survived by his eldest son
Who inherited his father's diary, locked in a cabinet for many years
Until a young woman implored to see the writings

And who came back day after day
Convinced, Niklas's son produced a key,
Opened the cabinet and a new chapter was born.

NIKLAS exits.

LITTLE MEI   My friend, thank you for helping us and for trying to tell people what happened here in Nanking.

Signed,

Little Mei,
Born in Shanghai
Abandoned at age five
Schooled and clothed by the Sisters of St. Marguerite
Walked from Shanghai to Nanking to escape the Japanese
Captured, raped and left for dead, December 1937
Survived.

LITTLE MEI exits.

2005

A year or so after the events of Act One.

Backstage. A lecture hall. An assembled crowd. JULIA, dressed nicely, is waiting.

AUDREY enters. She looks different than when we last saw her. Her spine is straighter, her clothes somehow more grown-up. She is carrying a garish diaper bag, a purse and raincoat.

JULIA   Audrey!

AUDREY   I'm sorry, Julia, there was so much traffic.

JULIA   They're just about to announce you.

AUDREY remembers the diaper bag.

AUDREY   Oh no, can you give this to the babysitter? They're in the green room, I think.

JULIA   Okay, no worries. Here, let me take the rest of this…

AUDREY   Thanks…

Beat.

JULIA   Are you ready?

AUDREY   Yeah, I mean, sure, yeah, no.

JULIA   You'll do fine.

AUDREY   It's just… I know it's what she would've wanted, but… I'm not Irene.

JULIA   She's already won the award! You could hardly screw it up now! Don't screw it up.

AUDREY   Julia!

JULIA   Just read it and you'll be fine. You'll be fine.

AUDREY   Thank you.

AUDREY crosses to a gentle spot. She is carrying a book. She takes a deep breath, trying to compose herself. From the wings, we hear a small baby gurgle. AUDREY takes a quick glance into the wings and that is the strength that she needed. She opens the book and looks out to the world.

"*The Nanking Incident*
By Irene Wu.

Chapter One.
1937. It was winter in Nanking…"

Lights.

The End.

Marjorie Chan is an acclaimed theatre artist, librettist and playwright based out of Toronto. Her play *China Doll* was nominated for Outstanding New Play and Outstanding Production at the Dora Awards, was a finalist for the 2005 Governor General's Literary Award and was performed in Hong Kong as part of Festival Canada Hong Kong. Her other works include *The Madness of the Square, Sanctuary Song, Persephone Calling, Mother Everest* and *in the garden, two suns*, an adaptation of Hisashi Inoue's celebrated play about Hiroshima.

Marjorie has been Playwright-in-Residence for Theatre Direct Canada as well as Playwright-in-Residence and Associate Artistic Director for Cahoots Theatre Projects. In addition to her writing and performing, Marjorie runs Crossing Gibraltar, a theatre training and outreach program for youth from refugee backgrounds. She is a graduate of George Brown Theatre School.